REINVENTING
DELL

Originally printed in paperback
by CreateSpace in November 2015.
First eBook edition distributed November 2015.

10 9 8 7 6 5 4 3 2 1

ISBN: 978-0-9948906-0-3

eISBN: 978-0-9948906-1-0

Edited by Katie Meyer.
Graphics by Heather Simmons.
Cover design and illustration by Dushan Milic.

For TT. So glad you stuck your head over the top of the cube.

REINVENTING DELL

Heather Simmons

MURMUROUS PUBLISHING
TORONTO, ONTARIO

Contents

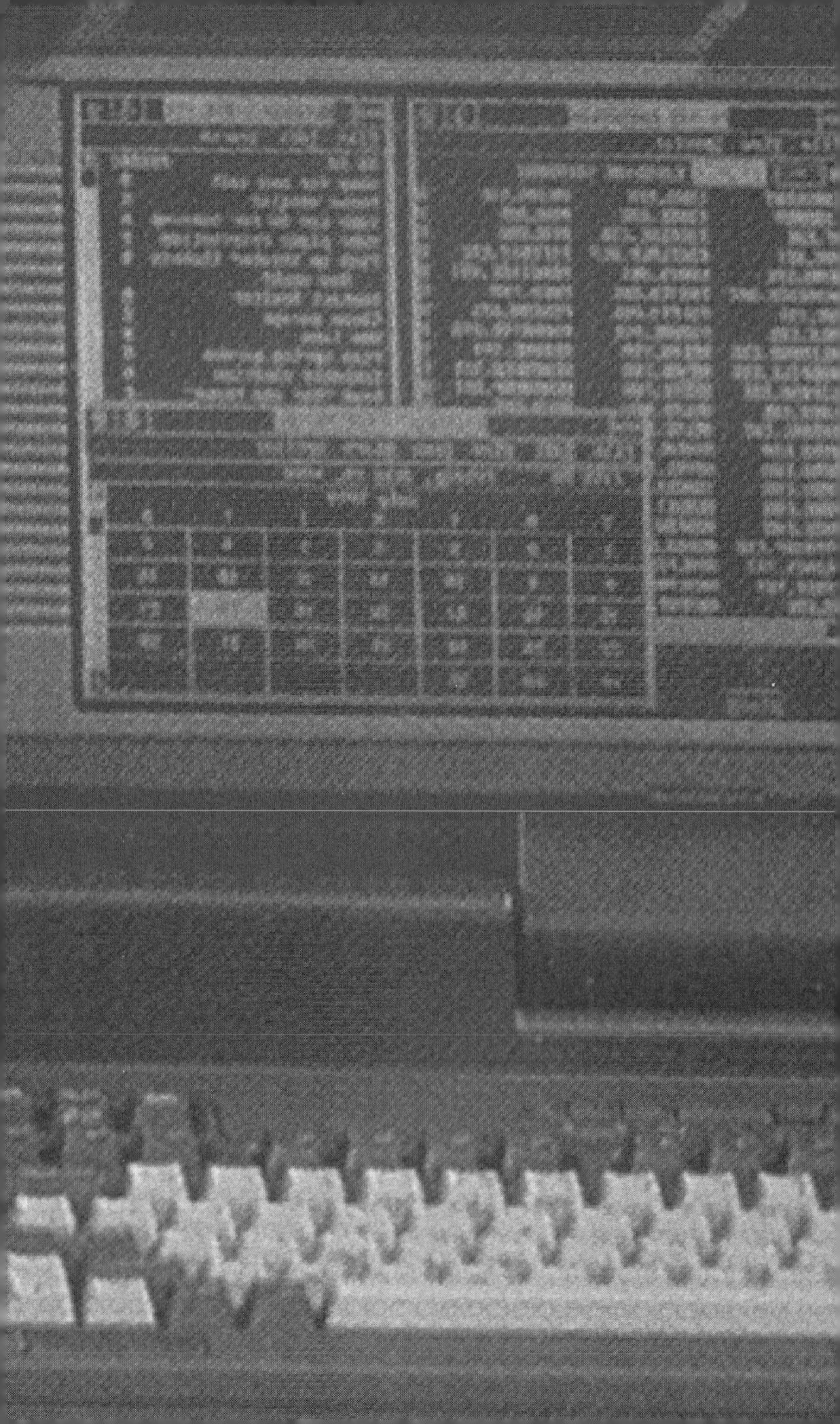

"There's no way. Who's going to buy a computer over the phone? They're complicated."

—Bill Sharpe, former CEO, Sharpe Blackmore

Introduction

To the disrupters go the spoils. Those who disrupt their industries change consumer behavior, alter economics, and transform lives. Companies can disrupt by creating revolutionary new technologies, as Corning Glassworks and Bell Labs did with the invention of fiber-optic cables in 1970,[1] or via design, as Apple did with its various "i" products. Or a company can disrupt with a revolutionary business model, as Dell did in the 1980s with the idea of selling $2,500 computers over the phone. But it wasn't just the business model that made Dell so disruptive.

When I graduated from Harvard Business School ("HBS") in 1990, one of my professors – the late Louis "By" Barnes – asked why I didn't stay to get my PhD in Organizational Behavior ("OB"). *OB??? No way! Not the soft stuff,* I thought. I was $40,000 in debt and needed to make money. Besides, weren't people interchangeable, as long as the numbers were there? Thus demonstrating (and not for the first nor last time) that 27-year-olds do not, in fact, know everything. I worked at Dell from 1992 to 2005. Dell's success was not only driven by its innovative direct business model, but also by the "soft stuff" – culture and employee commitment.

Fast forward 25 years, when my primary thesis advisor for my second master's degree, Suzanne Stein, said, "You have to write your thesis on Dell, innovation, and disruption. You're the only one who can tell that story." Well, maybe not the only one, but there are admittedly not many folks who studied innovation and culture at Harvard and McKinsey & Co., then worked for over a decade for Dell, before returning to school at the age of fifty to study innovation in the digital era. So I wrote my thesis on how innovative cultures are created, lost, and reborn in large organizations, through the lens of my Dell experience. And rather than leave it in a dusty academic archive where exactly three people might read and benefit from it, I've turned it into this book.

The book itself is powered by both the hard stuff and the soft stuff. It is largely based on interviews conducted over the past two years with ten former Dell employees (who worked there at various points between the mid-'80s and mid-2000s), to whom I am most grateful.

In Chapter 1, Revolutionary Performance, and Chapter 2, The Direct Model, we crunch the numbers on Dell's end-to-end performance and the business model that drove that performance. Chapter 3 details why innovation is more imperative than ever in the digital age, and Chapter 4 reviews a framework for producing innovative cultures in companies large and small, from the co-authors of the 2014 book *Collective Genius* from Harvard Business Review Press. Chapters 5 and 6 return to the story of Dell's rise through the '90s and subsequent struggle in the mid-2000s, told from the perspective of the ten former Dell employees, who ranged from VPs to front-line managers and from human resources professionals to operations gurus. It includes the views of Dell leaders such as former Vice President of Marketing Tom Martin. Among other observations, Tom noted that Dell's great strength – a relentless focus on executing its direct business model – led to the development of an "anti-innovation culture" over time. Chapter 7, Reinvention, introduces a new framework for managing innovation through acquisition in large organizations: the Intelligent Gambler©. In this chapter we also run the numbers on the likely outcome of Michael Dell's efforts to radically remake his company from a public purveyor of hardware devices to a private provider of end-to-end computing services. Chapter 8 concludes with a few suggestions of my own, as Dell reinvents itself as a private company.

Enough about how this book is organized. We return now to the beginning, and to Dell.

Truth be told, nobody thought Dell's direct business model would work, at least back in the early '90s. As Bill Sharpe, head of the advertising agency that held the Dell Canada account from 1996 to 2006, told me, "I had a business partner in California who said, 'We have a client, Dell. It sells computers over the phone and ships them to you.' I said, 'There's no way. Who's gonna buy a computer over the phone? They're complicated.'"

Bill's position was quite logical. In 1992, the year I joined the company, Dell had a 3.5% share of global personal computer ("PC") revenues, to IBM's dominant 12.4%.[2] The internet was used by almost no one outside of nerdy academic circles, e-commerce was five years away, and eventual Amazon founder Jeff Bezos was still working at financial firm D. E. Shaw.

Nobody thought the direct business model would work. But work it did, and spectacularly. Until it didn't. And therein lies the tale.

"A $10,000 investment in Dell at its 1988 initial public offering would have yielded a fortune of ~$6 million at the stock's peak."

—Heather Simmons

ONE

Revolutionary Performance

THE COMBINATION OF THE DIRECT business model and a risk-taker's culture produced one of the most successful businesses of the twentieth century. While Dell's growth stalled for several years in the mid-2000s, its end-to-end performance is the stuff of business school legend. From inception in 1984 to the fall of 2013, Dell generated about $800 billion in cumulative revenues, according to its annual reports. Annual sales grew at a torrid clip for its first twenty years. As shown in Figure 1.1, from 1991 to 2005, annual sales grew at a compound annual growth rate ("CAGR") of over 34%. Between 2005 and 2012, however, the CAGR slowed to .3%.

Dell's profit performance is no less impressive. Michael Dell started the company in his University of Texas college dorm room in 1984. By 1998, Dell was generating over $1 billion in profits every year, putting some serious daylight between itself and its competitors.

1

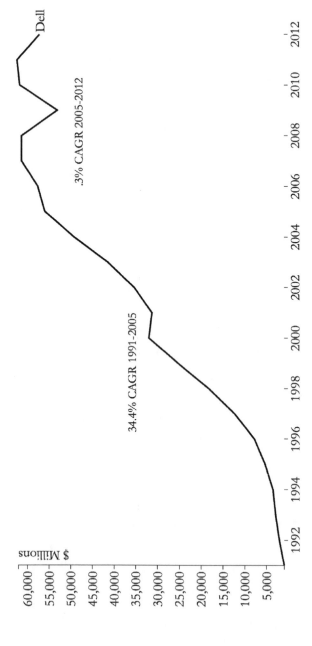

Figure 1.1. *Dell's annual revenues, 1991-2012.*[1]

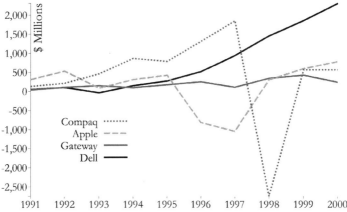

Figure 1.2. *Net income by major PC competitor,*
1991-2000.[1]

Through 2005, Dell's unit growth rate also
consistently outpaced the market, leading it to the
#1 market share position worldwide. However, by
2006 Dell's unit growth had slowed substantially. In
2007, Hewlett-Packard ("HP") surpassed Dell for the
#1 worldwide unit share position.

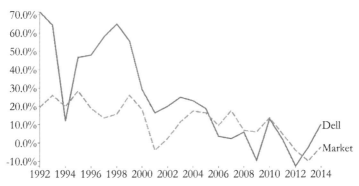

Figure 1.3. *Dell unit growth rates relative to*
market, 1992-2014.[2]

3

On a final measure, stock price, Dell also performed exceptionally well until about 2005. Cumulatively, it appreciated over 13,000% from its initial public offering ("IPO") in 1988 through October 2013 (just before it went private), yielding over *24 times* the return on the S&P 500 index.[3] Dell's annual return on equity from 1990 through 2012 averaged 42%, according to its annual reports.

Dell's stock performance during its heyday in the 1990s was even more impressive. The stock price climbed from about 10 cents a share at IPO to over $50 a share by the end of 1999.[3] Between December 1991 and December 1999, Dell's stock price appreciated by over 19,000%. No other competitor came close; HP was next with 900%.[3] Dell outperformed its next closest

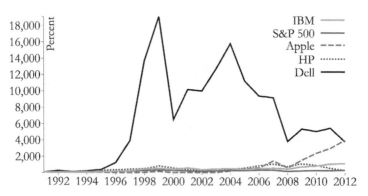

Figure 1.4. Dell's stock price performance relative to competitors, 1991-2012. December 31, 1991, stock price used as base and set to 100% for all competitors.[3]

competitor by a factor of over *twenty times* during the '90s.

Dell stock performance had a profound impact on the lives and fortunes of both employees and investors. A $10,000 investment in Dell at its 1988 initial public offering would have yielded a fortune of about $6 million at the stock's peak, Dell's valuation having risen by $100 billion in that time.[1,4]

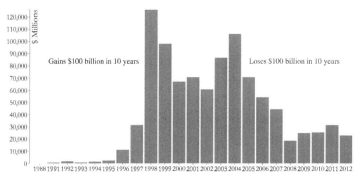

Figure 1.5. *Dell's stock market valuation, 1988-2012. Excludes debt.*[4]

Note: Dell's fiscal year ends January 31. Therefore, the 1998 valuation of $125 billion represents shares outstanding multiplied by stock price as of January 31, 1999, and so on.

Dell's unprecedented success did not go unnoticed. In 2005, Dell topped *Fortune*'s list of America's most admired companies. However, by the end of 2008, the stock was down to about $10, Dell had lost $100 billion in stock market value, Amazon was king of the direct distribution business, Apple had launched a slew of innovative consumer products including the iPhone, and Dell's low-cost advantage was under attack by Asian competitors. In 2013, Michael Dell and Silver Lake Partners took the company private for $24.9 billion, the 11th largest leveraged buyout ("LBO" – a transaction financed by significant debt) in history.[5]

One former Dell employee I interviewed asked, "How did Dell go from one of the most admired companies in the world to a cocktail party joke?" More importantly, how might it come back?

"The business model was the #1 driver of success. It was so **disruptive**. It defied logic."

—Bill Sharpe, former CEO, Sharpe Blackmore

TWO

The Direct Model

D ELL BECAME ONE OF THE most admired companies in the world due in large part to the revolutionary direct model that drove its exceptional end-to-end financial performance and formed the basis of its competitive advantage for decades. The direct model was pioneered by Michael Dell in his University of Texas dorm room in the early '80s. It was either brilliance on his part or simply necessity being the mother of invention: few established computer retailers were going to sell computers built by a kid in his dorm room. At least back in 1984.

In the classic indirect business model still used by HP, IBM, and most others in the PC industry, a computer manufacturer sells a limited set of standardized products through two layers of distribution, a distributor and a reseller (often referred to as "the channel"), in order to reach the end customer.

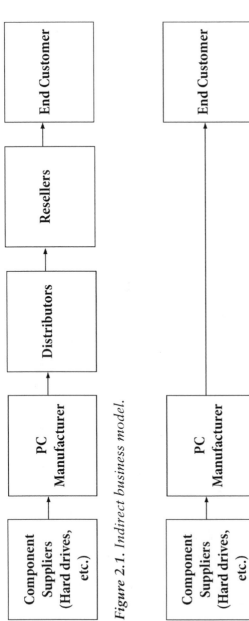

Figure 2.1. Indirect business model.

Figure 2.2. Direct business model.

By contrast, in the direct distribution or "build-to-order" model pioneered by Dell in 1984, the computer manufacturer does not build a product until a customer places an order. The manufacturer then ships a customized PC directly to the customer, bypassing the middleman.

The direct distribution model results in a value proposition for the customer of lower costs, customized products, faster time to market, and more accountable customer service. As calculated by technology analyst Steven Fortuna in 1997, the direct model provided Dell with a 14 point cost advantage over industry players with indirect models. Fortuna estimated that Dell saved 5% by avoiding the channel mark-ups, 4% due to higher inventory turns, 2.5% by avoiding price protection, and 2.5% through other items.[1] Dell then passed these lower costs to customers via lower prices. Fewer inventories (because Dell did not order parts until the end customer placed an order, and there was no inventory held by the reseller channel) also meant that Dell was typically two months faster to market with new products. Lower prices and newer products gave Dell an advantage during major product transitions such as Pentium.

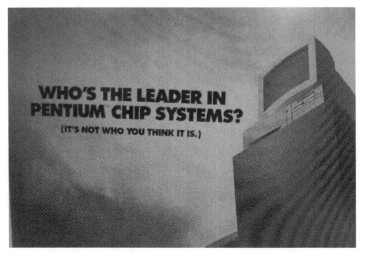

Figure 2.3. Dell ad from 1995 touting Pentium leadership, from the author's collection.

The direct business model also gave Dell one other critical advantage – higher cash flow due to an efficient cash conversion cycle,[2] sometimes referred to as *negative working capital*. The cash conversion cycle is calculated as days sales in receivables, plus days sales in inventory, less days sales in payables. A *negative* cash conversion cycle, which Dell had, means that a company is getting paid for sales faster than it is paying its suppliers (a good thing). Dell had less cash tied up in inventory than its indirect competitors, due to its model. In addition, Dell's customers – primarily businesses and governments – often paid Dell faster than it paid its own suppliers, meaning that less cash was tied up in accounts receivable.

Cash was therefore coming in much faster than it was going out. This was critical in Dell's early years, because it meant Dell could finance its phenomenal growth using other people's money. This advantage persists – Dell's most recent publicly available annual cash conversion cycle figure was a negative 36 days,[3] compared to a positive 6 days for IBM[4] and a positive 21 days for HP[5] for the closest equivalent period.

For more than twenty years, Dell's model provided it with lower costs and faster time to market. Then,

```
[575] From: Joel Kocher 1/26/94 3:03PM (3937 bytes: 45 ln)
To: Heather Simmons, Deborah Powell
Subject: Re: A PERFECT TEN
------------------------- Message Contents -------------------------
Proposed revision to Mike's "perfect 10" copy: Excellent!

"A PERFECT TEN!"

The Olympics, the symbol of the true competitive spirit,
rewards the very best with a perfect ten.  Dell is on the
threshold of completing our first ten years in business.
During this period, we first experienced phenomenal growth,
then, more recently, declining margins and competitive
pressures.  We got a "wake up call" in Q2 this year, when we
realized that we needed to develop our infrastructure to
support our growth.  Through this critical, cathartic year,
you have resolutely kept your eyes on the goal of "a perfect
ten."  Your persistence, determination, and guts have set us
up for "surthrival" in the 1990s and beyond.

The Circle of Excellence Program is designed to recognize
those of you who prove that you are the best of the best.
The President's Elite Award is your "perfect ten."  To
receive this award, you must make a conscious decision not
just to succeed, but to excel and drive Dell's future
success.

Your sales leadership will earn you the opportunity to
participate in our quarterly, semi-annual, and annual
awards, events, and trips.  It is entirely up to you!

This year is a turning point for Dell.  We will re-engineer
ourselves for a new competitive environment and a more
segmented market.  The challenges ahead are tremendous, and
I know that you will accept them with the same competitive
spirit you have shown this year.  You make the difference!

                                             Joel Kocher
```

Figure 2.4. "Surthrival" was first used in a motivational email to Dell's top salespeople in 1994.

in the mid-2000s, competitors began delivering more innovative products (such as tablets and smartphones) and services (such as security and cloud services), better design, and software. Innovation is Dell's best chance for "surthrival," a word coined by Dell's former president Joel Kocher in the early '90s (as seen in Figure 2.4). Surthrival means to not just survive, but to thrive.

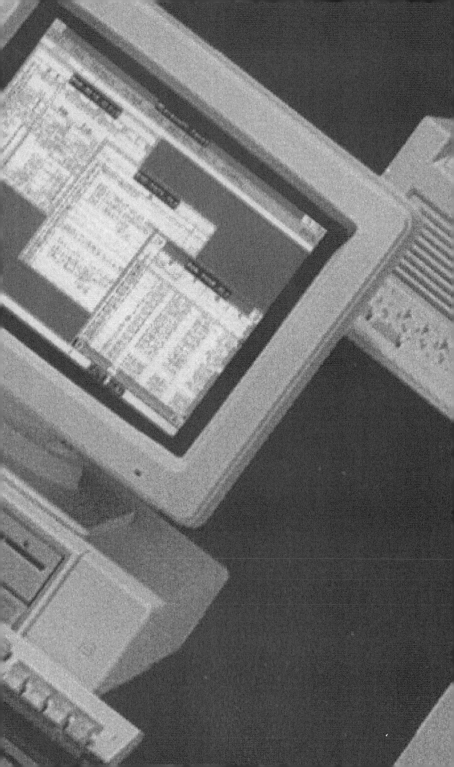

"Gentlemen, we have run out of money. It is time to start thinking."

—Sir Ernest Rutherford

THREE

The Innovation Imperative

L ET'S TALK ABOUT THE THEORY behind innovation before we get back to telling Dell tales. This part gets a wee bit academic, so if you're not into that, go grab yourself a cold one and rejoin us in Chapter 5.

Why should Dell, or any large company, care about this squishy concept called "innovation"? Isn't it just yet another buzzword, manufactured by academics and consultants?

Actually, no. Innovation is vital to Dell's surthrival. The pace of change in high technology is ever accelerating, requiring the integration of new technologies and combinations thereof far more often than ever before in our history. Innovation is vital for Dell, and for the high-tech industry in general.

More broadly, innovation is vital to prosperity, of nations and of individuals. Nobel Laureate Sir Ernest Rutherford once said, "Gentlemen, we have run out of money. It is time to start thinking."[1] In his book *Capitalism, Socialism, and Democracy*, Joseph Schumpeter identifies "creative destruction," or innovation that both creates new companies and destroys old ones, as the driving force of capitalism.[2] Schumpeter believed this creative destruction causes continuous progress and improves standards of living.

More modern scholars, economists, and business leaders concur with Schumpeter. According to a 2005 report called "Rising Above the Gathering Storm," prepared for the presidents of the National Academy of Sciences, National Academy of Engineering, and Institute of Medicine, 85% of the increase in per capita income in the US can be attributed to disruptive innovation.[3] The "Gathering Storm" committee, led by former Lockheed Martin CEO Norman Augustine, concludes that the engine of the future economy and job creation will be innovation, particularly in the sciences and engineering.[4] The "Gathering Storm" report goes on to cite several disturbing facts regarding where and how research and development ("R&D") dollars are being invested, notably that a) GE now has the majority of its R&D personnel outside the US, b) 77% of global firms planning to build R&D centers will do so in China or India, and c) US consumers spend more on potato chips than the US government spends on energy R&D.[5]

So innovation is vital to a strong economy, and to our standard of living. But what do we mean by innovation? As Harvard Business School professor Linda Hill and her co-authors say in their 2014 book, *Collective Genius*:

> Innovation is the creation of something both novel and useful ... It can be a new product, a new service, a new *business model* [emphasis added], a new way of organizing, or a new film made in a new way.[6]

I add that an innovation is something that is launched or introduced into the marketplace or culture. Inventions not introduced to the market are science experiments.

HBS professor Clayton Christensen, a leading innovation scholar, discussed disruptive innovation in his foundational 1997 text *The Innovator's Dilemma*:

> Disruptive technologies bring to a market a very different value proposition than had been available previously. Generally, disruptive technologies underperform established products ... But they have other features that a few fringe (and generally new) customers value ... disruptive technologies are typically cheaper, simpler, smaller, and frequently, more convenient to use.[7]

For example, small smart cars are disruptive to the automotive industry. Small transistors were a disruptive technology, rendering huge vacuum tubes redundant. Drone delivery of packages is disruptive to Canada Post (lots of things could be disruptive to Canada Post, which seems to have a delivery schedule generated by a random algorithm, but I digress).

Christensen also identified a different type of innovation, sustaining innovation, which typically improves the performance of existing established products in mainstream markets. In addition, he defined efficiency innovation, which involves reducing costs through simplified delivery or processes.[8]

I do not think Dr. Christensen's definition of disruptive technologies is completely adequate today. It implies an inferior but "good enough" product creeping into the bottom of a market, at a cheaper price than the existing offering. Today, technology often allows us to create superior products that leapfrog existing market offerings (e.g., the impact of Pixar and its CGI magic on the movie industry). Therefore, I prefer the definition of disruptive technologies posited by McKinsey, one of the world's foremost management consulting companies. McKinsey views a disruptive technology as one with a broad scope of impact (billions of people), significant economic value (trillions of dollars of revenue), and disruptive economic power (i.e., the potential to create winners and losers).[9] McKinsey includes next-generation genomics, the Internet of Things, and advanced energy storage as disruptive technologies. These technologies do not underperform existing technologies.

As noted by Dr. Hill and her co-authors in *Collective Genius*, disruption does not have to come from a technology or product alone. Disruptive innovation can also occur in the form of a new service or a new business model.

This disruptive innovation is more important to business success than it ever has been. In extended periods of rapid change, innovation is critical, and sustained innovation is, as the authors of *Collective Genius* say, "perhaps the only enduring competitive advantage."[10] The current digital wave of innovation spawned by the internet is far more rapid than that brought on by the Industrial Revolution of the late 1700s, which brought us the steam engine and ignited the rapid and sustained acceleration of innovation. It is also faster than the wave of innovation brought on by the internal combustion engine in the late 1800s. As an example, while it took electricity 45 years to reach 90% of US residents, it took cell phones just 20 years to reach that penetration.[11]

What is it about digital technologies in particular that causes this acceleration? MIT professors Erik Brynjolfsson and Andrew McAfee, in their book *The Second Machine Age*, suggest that the accelerated pace of the digital revolution is driven by three factors: exponential improvement, digitized information, and recombinant innovation.

One example of exponential improvement is high technology's well-known Moore's Law, first described by Intel co-founder Gordon Moore in 1965. Moore's Law states that "the complexity for minimum component costs has increased at a rate of roughly a factor of two per year."[12] In other words, the amount of hardware computing power you can get for a dollar doubles every year. In terms we can all understand, if you put a dollar in the bank and applied Moore's Law to it, you'd have $16 million to retire on in 25 years. Whoa, everybody just woke right up.

Figure 3.1. *Moore's Law applied to retirement savings, as calculated by the author.*

Moore's Law means that today's Sony PlayStation 3 has the same processing speeds as the world's fastest supercomputer in 1996.[13] Today's iPhone is also faster than a $10 million supercomputer of the 1970s.[14]

The second factor in the digital revolution, digitized data, has two important properties: it is non-rival, and costs to reproduce and distribute it are negligible. Non-rival means that something is not used up when it gets used, such as when I listen to a song on an iPod.[15]

The final factor is recombinant innovation, which simply means that most innovations in the digital age are new combinations of existing innovations, packaged together to solve a new problem. Steven Johnson takes the long view on this concept in his 2014 book, *How We Got to Now: Six Innovations That Made the Modern World*. As one example, Johnson begins his story of glassmaking innovation back in 1204, when Constantinople fell. A group of Turkish glassmakers fled to Venice, where the townspeople banished them to the island of Murano. During the 15th century, one of these glassmakers, Angelo Barovier, created clear glass by combining seaweed ash with molten glass. In the same century, Gutenberg produced the printing press, causing literacy rates to rise dramatically, and many people realized they were farsighted. That created demand for spectacles, for which, fortunately, there now existed clear glass. Fast forward about 400 years to 1887, when an eccentric professor named Charles Vernon Boys wanted to create a very fine strand of glass to measure the effects of delicate force on objects. So he did what any of us would do and attached molten glass to a crossbow, and then fired a shot across his lab, creating a very thin, long strand of clear glass. Almost 100 years later, Corning advanced both Boys' thin strands of glass and Barovier's transparency process to create fiber optics. The backbone of the global internet is built out of fiber optic cables.[16]

So if you like your internet connection robust, thank Gutenberg, the bureaucrats of Venice, and an eccentric professor with a crossbow. Innovations build on prior innovation, sometimes 100 years old. We all stand on the shoulders of giants. Please remember this the next time you think you invented social networks, or the internet, or crowdsourcing.

"**Big companies have the fulcrum. Innovation can be their lever.**"

—Scott Anthony,
Harvard Business Review blogs

FOUR

A Brief Sojourn in Academia

IN THE INTRODUCTION, I MENTIONED that this book is based on my master's thesis, completed at Ontario College of Art and Design University ("OCADU") in 2015. Generally, I find academia too… well, theoretical, and not so useful in analyzing the decisions made under the pressure of the real corporate world. The corporate world is also greatly influenced and driven by culture – something that is hard to capture in an academic "framework." While writing my thesis, however, I did in fact discover one academic framework that was quite useful when analyzing shifts in Dell's culture and performance.

For anyone who dislikes academic frameworks, I sympathize. Frameworks generally consist of a variety of geometric shapes, usually accompanied by arrows pointing out some interesting bits. They are often far too complicated to be remembered or useful in the heat of real-world business decision-making. Too much time is spent trying to make sure one has filled out every box, slot, circle, or doo-hickey, resulting in… stuff we already know. Time that could be better spent making something happen. I come by my aversion to frameworks honestly, having spent two years as an associate at McKinsey, the aforementioned consulting company. As author Duff McDonald writes of McKinsey in his book *The Firm*, "By the end of the 1980s, the firm required that new recruits learn more than a dozen core analytical frameworks, ranging from 'the raider's perspective' to return-on-equity trees, business systems, industry cost curves, value-delivery systems, economic value to the shareholder, and the strategic game board … The real ball-busters … were heavy on the numbers, from cost of capital to returns on all manner of investments."[1] He got that right, except it was more than fifty frameworks; we had a whole book of frameworks. And now you know why I hate them.

Anyway, my thesis advisors Eric Blais and Suzanne Stein insisted on a framework for my thesis, so I searched for one I could stand. The search brought me, paradoxically, all the way back to HBS, circa 1990. The spring before I graduated, I took another OB class, taught by a new professor named Dr. Linda Hill. In 1990, we MBA students were all in our mid-20s, and the rumour was that Dr. Hill was not much older. She was young, tall, commanding, and intimidatingly smart. Dr. Hill scared the heck out of me most days. She usually appeared mildly bemused by my in-class comments (I was prone to outbursts like "Life's too short to develop people!" back then).

Fast forward to 2014, when Dr. Hill and her co-authors created a new framework for building an innovative culture, as described in their book, *Collective Genius*. It appealed to me for its simplicity, and because the elements of the framework were illustrated with real-world examples. According to Hill and her co-authors, in order to build an innovative organization, leaders must create an environment in which employees are both willing and able to innovate.[2] To create an organization that is willing to innovate, a company needs a purpose, shared values, and rules of engagement. To build an organization able to innovate requires three capabilities: creative abrasion (creating a multitude of options through debate and discussion), creative agility (experimenting quickly and changing directions as required), and creative resolution (the ability to make integrative decisions that build on the options rather than "either or" decisions that simply pick one).[3] We'll discuss each element of this framework in turn and provide a real-world example to show it in action.

WILLING TO INNOVATE   ABLE TO INNOVATE

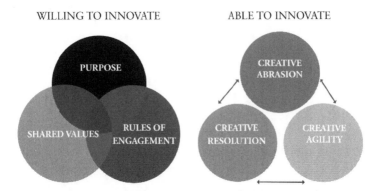

Figure 4.1. Author's drawing of Hill, et al.'s Willing and Able to Innovate framework.[3]

PURPOSE

Let's review the elements of the "Willing" side of the framework first. A great example of "purpose" comes from Tim Brown's 2008 article, "Design Thinking." According to Brown, the stated purpose of India's Aravind Eye Care System (one of the world's largest providers of eye care) is to eradicate blindness in India, including among the rural poor.[4] That is surely a vision that inspires its employees, who provide care to more than 2 million patients a year, 60% of whom cannot afford to pay.

SHARED VALUES AND RULES OF ENGAGEMENT

Hill and her co-authors use Pixar to illustrate how

"shared values" and "rules of engagement" could be used to create some of the most innovative movie experiences ever. Pixar utilized daily reviews that encouraged individual contributions from all members of a film's team. Pixar had open and non-hierarchical communication (a shared value) – anyone could give the director comments about the production.[5] There was, however, some structure (rules of engagement). People were encouraged to innovate, experiment, and fail – but the film's release deadline had to be met, and financial data such as shots per week were tracked religiously. In addition, while all team members were encouraged to make suggestions and participate in debates, the director retained full creative control, making the final decisions.[6] Beyond these guardrails and end goals, structure was used sparingly.

CREATIVE ABRASION

Moving on to the "Able" side of Hill's framework, the need for creative abrasion, or rich, diverse ideas competing through discourse and debate,[7] is well established both by other scholars and by real-world examples. Min Basadur, for example, emphasizes the need to create intellectual diversity by ensuring teams have a mix of personality types: generators, conceptualizers, optimizers, and implementers.[8] (You may not have heard of this work unless you enjoy perusing scholarly databases for gripping titles such as *Creative Problem-Solving Process Styles, Cognitive Work Demands, and Organizational Adaptability*).

Basadur, et al., posit that organizations that value diversity of thought in their organizations enable the "creative abrasion" Hill refers to in her framework. Other scholars noting the importance of constructive conflict between diverse individuals include Bruce Tuckman, who produced the Forming, Storming, Norming, and Performing framework to describe effective team dynamics.[9]

Creative abrasion is also fostered by diverse backgrounds and personalities, which will be important when we return to Dell's culture. In *The Innovators*, Walter Isaacson introduces Stewart Brand, an oddball event producer who took LSD and helped create the hippie counterculture in California in the late '60s.[10] Brand produced the 1966 Trips Festival, hosted by Ken Kesey, founder of a hippie commune who was out on bail after a drug bust. The festival was a unique fusion of drugs, music (Big Brother and the Holding Company, the Grateful Dead), and technology (strobe lights, sci-fi movies, gadgets, and pinball). Douglas Engelbart, a smart, monotone engineer who "sometimes gave the impression he had not been born on this planet" took notice.[11] Engelbart ran the Augmentation Research Center (studying augmented intelligence) just down the street from one of Brand's ventures. The two teamed up in 1968 for a demo of Engelbart's "oNLine System," a precursor to the PC, with its mouse, graphics display, document sharing, and email capabilities. The "Mother of all Demos" featured Engelbart's computer display projected on a large screen at a computer conference. Brand worked the cameras and selected images for display on Engelbart's computer from 30 miles away, connected via leased microwave lines. They created a sensation by collaborating remotely to create and edit a document, embed audio and video, and create hypertext links. The demo kickstarted the development of the PC. Even Ken Kesey was impressed, noting that the personal computer was "the next thing after acid."[12]

Creative abrasion among team members with diverse skill sets and personalities is necessary for innovation. It helps to have a few brainy nerds with questionable personalities. It helps to have an oddball or two. Drugs may or may not be necessary or condoned by the human resources department.

CREATIVE AGILITY

Creative agility is the ability to experiment and

use the data from those experiments to pivot (shift directions) when needed. Tim Brown, CEO of award-winning global design firm IDEO, promotes experimentation using the term "ideation."[13] Through ideation, designers and makers rapidly prototype new ideas and get those prototypes out into the hands of real users. Data and observations of potential customers actually using the prototypes can often produce pivots, or changes in direction, as usage in the "field" is often different than use in the "lab." Peter Senge, author of *The Fifth Discipline: The Art and Practice of the Learning Organization,* supports the gathering of data from real-world experiments in order to remain agile. According to Senge, the discipline of "mental models" is to sift out the actual data that supports or dismantles the assumptions we have about the real world.[14] If our mental models aren't based on real data, we will produce products or services that don't meet real customer needs.

Examples of real-world pivots that spur innovation abound. Groupon – the site that issues coupons if a certain number of your friends sign up to buy the same product or service – started life as an activism hub (e.g., schedule a rally of 100 people in the town hall). Vital Alert Communication, a small underground communications company I ran, started life making voice-to-voice communications gear for mines, subways, and tunnels. After numerous tests in subways and tunnels, we determined that text-based communication and binary communications (yes/no, on/off) were much more reliable underground and began developing products that emphasized data communication over voice.

CREATIVE RESOLUTION

Hill and her co-authors describe creative resolution as integrating ideas to create a solution that is better than the alternatives on the table. Roger Martin, former dean of the Rotman School of Business at the University of Toronto, is often quoted on this topic. He describes the "opposable mind," which he defines as the ability to hold two conflicting ideas in a constructive tension that induces the synthesis of new and superior ideas. The solution contains elements of opposing ideas (and perhaps a new innovation or relaxed constraint) but is superior to each.[15] Rather than simply choosing between option A or option B based on an analysis of the current data, leaders of innovation must seek superior alternatives that combine elements of both options. Moreover, leaders cannot simply assume existing constraints (such as battery life, for example) will hold for long in the exponential acceleration of the digital age.

The creation of ARPAnet, the predecessor to the internet, provides a real-world example of the power of creative resolution and opposable minds. (ARPA is the Defense Department's Advanced Research Projects Agency.) As described by Walter Isaacson in his book *The Innovators*, Larry Roberts and Bob Taylor invited their fellow ARPA researchers to a meeting in 1967, where Roberts described two possibilities for creating a shared network of research computers. A year before Brand and Englebart stunned by demonstrating remote communication between two computing devices, computers were only available at large government and research institutions and were not connected to one another. Larry Roberts's first option was a hub and spoke system, with a centralized "big node" that routed information. His second was a web of equally powerful, decentralized nodes connected to each other. The other researchers objected to Roberts's preferred decentralized network option. They argued that their large computers were already at capacity and could not afford the additional "load" of acting as a node in a network, routing information to the right place. Wes Clark, a Lincoln Laboratory researcher, developed an idea superior to either of the options: the use of a router. A router routes data between nodes on a network, based on a standard, pre-established protocol. In ARPAnet, a router moved data between the large research computers, which were then able to both retain their full capacity and be connected to other computers in a decentralized network.[16] This was clearly superior to either of the two alternatives presented to the researchers.

The previous paragraphs described groups that were successful in creating the willingness and ability to innovate. What happens if an organization does not foster this willingness and ability? Patrick Lencioni describes it well in his book *The Five Dysfunctions of a Team*. A lack of trust, fear of conflict, lack of commitment, avoidance of accountability, and inattention to results can undermine both sides of Hill's innovation framework.[17] A fear of conflict prevents creative abrasion, and lack of trust and commitment prevent creative resolution. Avoidance of accountability and inattention to results lead to a hesitance to pivot (creative agility) when results indicate a need to do so. According to Lencioni, the upshot of the five dysfunctions is a team dominated by status and ego, pursuing ambiguous goals in pursuit of low standards (and thus results), in an environment of artificial harmony. In short, a team treading water to maintain an unsatisfactory status quo.

The literature is also full of high-profile examples

of companies that failed to innovate. In his book
How the Mighty Fall, Jim Collins cites Motorola,
which in 1995 introduced the StarTac phone – the
smallest such phone to date – with a cool clamshell
design. The only trouble was, the phone was analog,
and carriers were beginning to demand digital. But
Motorola, the market leader, assumed its millions of
analog customers couldn't be wrong. The company
tried to dictate the share of carrier sales that had to
be Motorola. Carriers resisted this arrogance, and
Motorola's share fell from nearly 50% to just 17% by
1999.[18] Clayton Christensen, in his second book *The
Innovator's Solution*, describes how integrated steel
giants such as Bethlehem Steel were disrupted by steel
mini-mills.[19] The mini-mills required considerably less
capital investment. Mini-mills simply melt existing
scrap metal in electric arc furnaces, in contrast to
the steel producers who create and purify steel from
iron ore, coke, and limestone in a two-stage process.
Mini-mill steel was lower quality and also 20%
lower cost, so mini-mills initially targeted the market
for construction rebar (i.e., steel bars that reinforce
concrete), where fit and finish were less important.
The steel giants did not react, as this market was
their lowest margin business. Bethlehem Steel closed
its last structural beam plant in 1995, conceding to
the mini-mills.[20] Whether through arrogance or blind

pursuit of profits, these companies failed to pivot and innovate when necessary.

The literature also has stories of once-innovative large brands that lost their innovation edge, and came back. Crest, for example, was the market leader in toothpaste until the late 1990s, when it dropped to the #2 slot behind Colgate. It stormed back in the mid-2000s with innovations in teeth whitening and oral health.[21] There is also, of course, Apple, which emerged from near bankruptcy to unleash a torrent of innovative "i" products when Steve Jobs returned to the company after a 12-year absence in 1997.

Apple is an example of an organization in which the leader had a disproportionate impact on the ability of an organization to innovate. What is the role of the leader in creating an organization that is willing and able to innovate? During the Art of Leadership conference held in Toronto in November 2014, I asked Dr. Hill what had been the decade's biggest change in innovation thinking. She said, "It is the shift from economics to ecosystem. Twenty to thirty years ago, most of the people studying innovation were economists – like Christensen. They were interested in the economic impact of innovation. Today, it is much more about how to create the ecosystem and the culture that supports innovation." Leaders seeking to establish a culture in which employees are willing to innovate also tend to "lead from behind," as Hill puts it. Vineet Nayar, CEO of Indian high-tech firm HCL Industries (which successfully transitioned from hardware to services between 2008 and 2013), says:

> Leaders must avoid the urge to answer every question or provide a solution to every problem. Instead you must start asking questions, seeing others as the source of [innovation] ... The greatest impact is that it unleashes the power of the many and loosens the stranglehold of the few, thus increasing the speed and quality of innovation and decision making ... every day.[22]

Stephen Covey, author of *Principle-Centered Leadership,* describes this concept as "self-directed work teams."[23] Employees on these teams are empowered and expected to solve problems, someway, somehow, and thus are both engaged and innovative.

Christensen notes that changes in leadership can result in markedly different innovation results, simply based on different problem-solving approaches employed by those leaders. For example, he states that from 1981 to 1999, Sony did not launch one new disruptive business. In the early 1980s, founder Akio Morita withdrew from day-to-day management of the company to become more active in politics.

In his place, the company brought in MBAs with sophisticated analytical tools. These analytical MBAs were able to identify some incremental opportunities in existing markets (i.e., sustaining innovations), but lacked the disruptive insights from observation and rapid prototyping – the creative spark – that Morita had championed.[24]

Leaders matter, and culture matters. The role of the leader in a time of exponential acceleration of innovation is to create a culture in which all team members are willing and able to innovate. The challenge, of course, is to sustain that innovative culture through the years as the company grows. And when you grow revenues close to 35% year on year for over a decade as Dell did, that challenge looms large. Do big companies like Dell even have a part to play in leading innovation, or should that be solely the province of Silicon Valley start-ups?

The structure and bureaucracy required to maintain a large company might seem to render innovation impossible. Scott Anthony, of the *Harvard Business Review*, notes, "Most people continue to believe big companies are where innovation goes to die."[25] Generating innovative ideas aside, can large companies even keep up? "This is the time for [IBM CEO Ginny] Rometty to prove wrong the thesis that large enterprises have no chance of surviving through innovation," Yale's Jeffrey Sonnenfeld says, in a recent *Fortune* article.[26] As early as 1934, economist Joseph Schumpeter said,

> New combinations are, as a rule, embodied, as it were, in new firms which generally do not arise out of the old ones but start producing beside them; to keep to the example already chosen, in general it is not the owner of stage-coaches who builds railroads.[27]

When start-ups like Instagram (2010) and Foursquare (2009) can appear and grow to over 1 million users in less than 24 months,[28] lumbering giants like Dell, GM, and IBM seem positively anachronistic, throwbacks to an earlier time before mobile phones and social media put the customer in control, turned millions into content creators, and spawned 13-year-old global pop stars from viral YouTube videos.

Nevertheless, it is worthwhile to assess whether large US-based corporations such as Dell can survive, and indeed, thrive, through innovation because large corporations have a) access to the capital needed to invest in innovation, and b) a *higher* tolerance for risk than smaller companies, simply because they have more substantial financial assets with which to absorb failure.

First, large corporations have access to the capital

needed to invest in innovation. This point was underlined by the near-catastrophic events of 2008-2009. In 2008, the global economy experienced a 100-year flood. The Great Recession was heralded by the unprecedented failure of Wall Street firm Lehman Brothers. That led to a one-day loss of over 500 points in the Dow Jones Industrial Average, which presaged a brutal decline of almost 50% in major stock averages over the next few months. Unemployment climbed to 10%, and the US government had to bail out home lenders Fannie Mae and Freddie Mac. The Great Recession wiped out retirement dreams. It also increased risk aversion among corporations, which began hoarding cash.[29] Banks tightened credit, and US venture capitalists ("VC"s) reduced financing by 40% following the collapse, from $32.1 billion to $20.4 billion (see Figure 4.2).[30]

Unlike VCs, large corporations had significant amounts of cash stockpiled during the recession, waiting to be deployed. Compare the balance sheets of America's large tech giants to the total US venture capital investment of $30 billion in 2013 (the last year for which Dell's cash balance is available). Microsoft ("MS") had $84 billion in cash in 2013, Google had $59 billion, Cisco had $47 billion, Apple had $41 billion,[31] and Dell had $12 billion. With

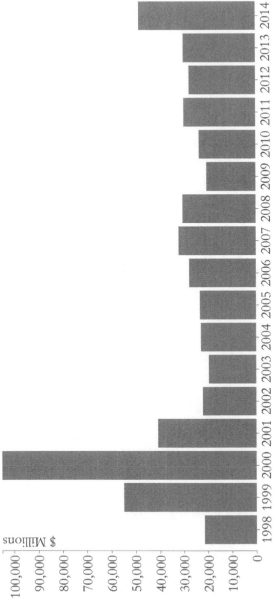

Figure 4.2. US venture capital investments by year, 1998–2014.[30]

interest rates now near zero, debt financing is also abundant and cheap. Corporations are awash in capital[32] and have greater capacity to innovate than small firms.

Second, scholars have found that large companies also have a higher tolerance for risk than small companies. This is counterintuitive to anyone who has worked in these large organizations. However, I believe this higher tolerance reflects the more significant assets large firms have, not a more entrepreneurial attitude among executives managing large core businesses. If Corporation X has $50 million in cash and Corporation Y has $250,000, I believe that Corporation X's managers will be more likely to invest $100,000 in a new venture, simply because one mistake is not "life threatening" to that corporation. Scholarly research supports this view. Michael Walls and James Dyer found risk tolerance increases with size, but at a decreasing rate.[33] They note that larger firms have more resources to absorb failure, learn from experiments, perfect the innovations of smaller companies, and pivot in new directions. Ronald Howard similarly found that corporate risk tolerance grew in proportion to financial measures such as sales and income.[34]

Other scholars, in contrast, note that there are certain factors that hold big businesses back from innovation once they hit a certain scale. For example, Robert Sutton and Huggy Rao, in their 2014 book *Scaling Up Excellence,* state,

> As organizations and programs expand and age, they often propagate ever more convoluted procedures and processes. Ballooning brigades of administrators must justify their existence. So they busy themselves by writing more rules and requiring colleagues to jump through more hoops – stealing bandwidth, effort, and willpower from more essential work.[35]

As companies grow, so does their structure; bureaucracy can paralyze a corporate culture. Jim Collins, in *How the Mighty Fall,* also describes obstacles that companies face as they try to scale up innovation. He cites an obsession with growth that sets up a vicious cycle of expectations (and I would add, reduces time available to experiment and innovate), a related declining proportion of the right people in key seats, problematic leader successions, and a shift in focus to reorganization and internal issues.[36]

In summary, large companies have the power to make significant changes by applying their considerable human and financial capital to global problems, if they can navigate through the scaling challenges that Collins, Sutton, and Rao describe.

Large firms are more resilient than smaller firms, for whom one mistake can be financially fatal. As Scott Anthony notes, "Big companies have the fulcrum. Innovation can be their lever."[37] Large companies can, and should, be leaders in this era of exponential innovation. This brings us back to the good stuff: the Dell story.

"A lot of people can put pretty plans in place, but they don't know how to execute. Dell did."

— former human resources director

FIVE

The Early Years

WE'LL START AT THE BEGINNING. During its
early years (roughly 1984 to 2000), Dell's
success was driven by four factors, according to
former employees: a) the direct business model, b)
entrepreneurial culture and commitment, c) risk-
taking, and d) leadership. These four elements created
a seemingly unstoppable machine that marched to a
#1 global market share.

Dell's direct business model was one of the
most significant sources of advantage. As Tom
Martin, former vice president of marketing, noted,
"The obvious thing is, Dell had a business model,
which led to a structural cost advantage that was
mathematically significant. A 10% or so cost
advantage, in a commodity business, is material,
especially when you're purchasing a lot. If you're
buying scotch tape, 60 cents vs. 66 cents for a roll
at Target does not change the purchase decision. If

you are spending $60 million, 10% is material. And
it was structural, so it was hard to copy – because
competitors had other business models, and felt
that they had to abandon those models in order to
pursue the direct model. And the gap out in cashflow
in that transition was too big, so they couldn't, or
thought they couldn't, copy it." Bill Sharpe, the
former CEO of Sharpe Blackmore, agreed when we
spoke in September 2014: "The business model was
the #1 driver of success. It was so disruptive. It defied
logic. Without the original business model and the
disruption it caused, you'd never have had a Dell –
you would have never gotten off the ground."

Michael Dell believed strong customer
relationships and the free flow of information were
the most valuable benefits of the direct model.[1] Dell
has shifted its business model to include the reseller
channel so that it may effectively target small to mid-
size businesses, and other competitors have increased
direct sales. Still, Dell sells 60% of its products
directly,[2] far more than other competitors.

Without the direct business model, Dell would
not have had a double-digit cost advantage or direct
relationships with customers. The model was crucial
to Dell's success.

The second factor in Dell's success, entrepreneurial
culture and commitment, drove the relentless

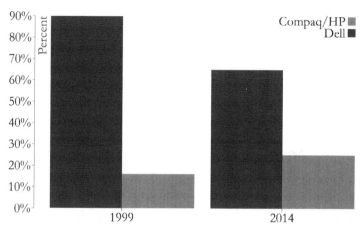

Figure 5.1. Direct sales percentage.[2,3,4,5]

execution that continually enhanced the advantages
of the direct model. In Hill's terms, entrepreneurialism
and commitment were two of Dell employees' shared
values.

One employee who worked in corporate services
told me that Dell's shared value of employee
commitment was even more important to its success
than the business model. "The direct business model
could have been anything – jeans that zip up in the
back, whatever. If you have leadership and employee
commitment, you can do anything," she said. "Each
quarter, the Dell leadership team would figure out
exactly what we needed to do this quarter, or for the
next two quarters. They would make it absolutely
clear. We would focus on that and we would just go

fucking do it. And that's exactly what would happen. There was leadership, and employee commitment, and people getting it done." Indraj Gill, a former marketing director in Asia Pacific and North America, told me, "Dell could have been built on selling pink Cadillacs – it was the entrepreneurial culture that made it work. And the leadership. Culture is #1 because that was what it was all about. You don't stay until 3:00 in the morning doing a price move just for money. That level of commitment doesn't happen for just a job. There is a culture of rewarding, intangibly and tangibly, risk-taking. Just do it. We all gave of ourselves. This culture came from Joel Kocher. It started from the top. The culture wasn't formalized. It was there because of certain individuals."

Joel Kocher, Dell's president of worldwide sales, marketing, and service, was indeed a force of nature. *Business Week* once called him a "marketing whiz whose needle is stuck on motivate." He was inspiring, charismatic, and most of all, intensely committed to success. He was also a showman – he drove racecars on stage, shaved his head, and wore camouflage, among other things, at Dell's all-employee conferences, which were pep rallies for grown-ups. And they worked. We were fired up and motivated to do "whatever it takes" to satisfy the customer and close the sale.

I was fortunate enough to work for Joel, as his executive assistant, from 1993 to 1994. One early morning in the spring of 1993, I was working away in my cricket-filled cube in a low-slung industrial building on Braker Lane in Austin (not for nothing did Dell have some of the lowest operating expenses in the industry). Suddenly, I heard, "Simmons! Do you have a minute to talk with me?" I turned around, wondering who the hell else was here at 7:30 AM, and saw that it was Joel (as I soon learned, he worked ten-plus hour days routinely). After telling me he was impressed with my launch of a new software business for Dell, he asked if I would like to be his executive assistant. Being an accountant, Harvard MBA, and introvert, I politely sat there quietly waiting for him to describe the responsibilities of the job, when it would start, and other details. After a moment, Joel gave me his deadpan stare and said, "I assume from your silence that you are simply thrilled with the idea." Laughing, I said yes.

Thus began one of the greatest adventures and learning experiences of my career. Joel mentored me in leadership and communication skills (unfortunately for those who worked for me, these were talents I perfected only decades later). I learned how to relate to other people from his administrative assistant Deborah Powell (and her equally able sidekick Carla

Hadley Thew), who was probably wiser and more intuitive than Joel and me put together. During that time, we opened offices in Europe (I once saw Joel walk off a nine-hour red-eye flight to Frankfurt and deliver a welcome speech to personnel in our new German office, his opening sentences in their language), hired new executives, and dealt with the problems of 50%+ year-on-year growth.

In the early '90s, these problems were legion. In the second quarter of 1993, Dell announced its first and only quarterly loss, of $76 million. The loss was attributed to a writeoff of Dell's line of notebook computers (Dell indeed scrapped all of its notebook products and boldly started over, under the leadership of John Medica, formerly of Apple), excess and obsolete inventory writeoffs, and restructuring of European operations. Dell had been overly focused on driving top-line revenue growth, at the expense of profits. Under the leadership of new chief financial officer ("CFO") Tom Meredith, the company wisely decided to prioritize liquidity and profits along with sales growth. This led to the development of Dell's mantra throughout the remainder of the 90s: "Liquidity, Profitability, Growth."

Tom Meredith was incredibly smart and, like many Dell executives, very accessible and quick to make decisions. In the summer of 1993, cash flow was very tight – for the aforementioned reasons. I had been assigned to lead a worldwide team to sell off about 30,000 units of excess and obsolete inventory, while Tom Meredith went in search of some bridge financing. The excess units were code-named Wildkitties. (To this day, Michael continues to allow hard-working engineers to name products as they launch. Good for morale but perhaps not so good for marketing or internal clarity.) We ran the numbers, and got approval to sell the obsolete units at 88 cents on the dollar, to whomever would take them. We tried many different promotions and tactics but still had most of the units left as the end of the summer approached. In late July 1993, I got a phone call at 8:30 in the morning from Henk Prenger, one of our sales managers in our Benelux office. He explained that he had a deal to sell all remaining Wildkitties to a retailer in Benelux but needed an answer within two hours, before the decision-maker left for a month-long European holiday. The price worked out to 87 cents on the dollar, below my approved limit. So, I told Henk I would call him back within half an hour. I phoned Tom's office, but got no answer, so I dashed out of my office, undoubtedly crushing a few crickets on the way. I hopped in my car and raced to Tom's office at the Arboretum (an actual office building, with elevators and no crickets, about ten minutes away). Out of breath, I told Tom's assistant that I needed to "speak with Tom, right NOW – about the Wildkitties."

Tom was in a meeting but immediately ushered his guest out of his office and waved me in.

"Tom, I have a deal for all of the Wildkitties, in Europe," I said, "but it's at 87 cents, so…"

He cut me off, responding, "Do it, go."

In less than 30 seconds, the decision was made, and millions of dollars of cash poured in by the end of the month. Crisis averted. Rapid-fire decision-making was a key element of Dell's entrepreneurial culture. Senior managers and bureaucracy did not get in the way of getting things done. (The stunning "all or nothing" disposition of the Wildkitties also led to one of my favorite Dell memories. At the weekly procurement/marketing meeting where I announced the news, Vice-President of Manufacturing Keith Maxwell double-clutched but then managed to get out a politically correct, "Atta… atta… PERSON!".)

One of the other elements of Dell's entrepreneurial culture was the employee commitment. The relative youth of Dell employees contributed to Dell's "work hard, play hard" culture. In 1993, the average age of a Dell employee was 28, the same age as Michael himself.[6] As one former employee recounted, "We just did what it took to get it done. We'd work 12-hour

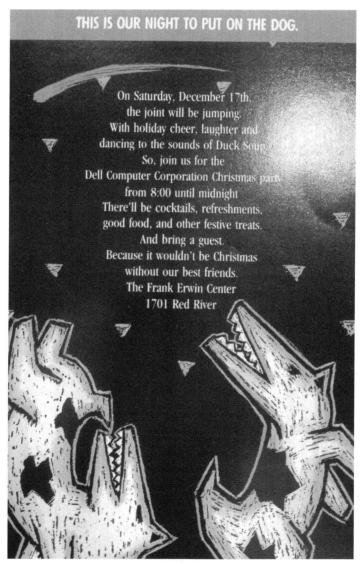

Figure 5.2. Dell holiday party invitation from the late '80s.

days, and then go to Trudy's for drinks and dancing, then get up at 6 AM and do it all again. We worked really hard. And played hard. One of our Christmas parties in the late '80s was held at the Frank Erwin Center, in Austin, a huge arena. We all still remember that party." (This was not the only memorable party. In one interview I learned that after-work drinks at Tangerines, a bar in the Aboretum office building, contributed to many a Dell workplace romance and a couple of marriages. I rarely missed a party but can't say I've ever been to Tangerines, so I will leave that to another storyteller.)

A former executive likewise recalls, "We were working 14 to 16 hours a day, and not feeling tired at the end of it. That was due to the employee commitment, and the leadership. There was such alignment between the top levels and the front-line employees. We were very aligned – amazingly aligned, actually."

Navigating the rapid change in the industry as Dell created it, following the lead of a visionary founder, all while growing at close to 50% year on year for the better part of the decade, did indeed lead to some long days. Most Dell employees I knew worked at least a sixty-hour week. Tom Martin, former VP of marketing and king of analogies, once described it as "trying to change the tires on a Ferrari while driving at 300 miles per hour."

While some might say this was an environment ripe for burnout, entrepreneurial employees seemed to understand that "start-ups" required hard work. They loved being the underdogs to the "corporate suits" just down the road in Houston (Compaq, which had the #1 market share) and knew it would be difficult to get the level of responsibility they had at such a young age anywhere else in the Fortune 500. Besides, we were both a belligerent upstart and one of the fastest-growing companies in the Fortune 500. Most of us knew we weren't in for a Junior League tea party.

We also used humor to break the tension. In 1994, I was promoted to director of the corporate desktop marketing team for North America. (The engineers named this product line "Optiplex" – I can't explain it either). During one quarter, when the Optiplex team was tasked with selling 195,000 desktops (nearly 50% year-on-year growth in a market growing in the low teens), team members repeatedly voiced their concerns that this goal was unattainable. I responded, "My mom could hit that number if she only came in on Tuesdays. And only worked at lunch hour." Team member Indraj Gill snuck into my office one day after the quarter ended, took a photo from my desk, and came back with some t-shirts for the team (Figure 5.3).

Figure 5.3. Front and back of desktop team's t-shirt, mid-'90s. Courtesy Indraj Gill.

Winning also inspired a lot of hard work.

A Human Resources director who worked at Dell in the early 2000s remembers that this level of employee commitment was not driven purely by financial incentives. She says, "If I were hiring today, I'd look for people with a bias towards action, who were collaborative and could learn on the fly. They have to have that commitment, and that is such a tough thing to test for. A lot of people are just looking for the next rung up, the next job, the next stock options." In contrast, she continues, "Dell was successful because people believed in it. People focused more on their jobs than the stock options. There was a difference, because the people that came in, the strategic guys, they all said, what can you do for me in stock options? And people like (names a number of engineers who had been there since the '90s) were the guys that didn't really care about that. And they were the guys working 16-to-18-hour days."

In sum, Dell's entrepreneurial culture included shared values of commitment, a bias towards action, and clear communication. As with Pixar, a flattened hierarchy and open communication style, matched with clear goals, created a culture that allowed innovation. Employees were also aligned around a common purpose: to topple Compaq for the #1 market share. This helped create an environment in which employees were willing to innovate.

The third factor in Dell's success is risk-taking, coupled with the resultant speed of execution. Part of this was driven by the company's non-hierarchical management structure, and part of it was ingrained in the people Dell hired, who preferred to beg forgiveness rather than ask permission – at least in the early days. A former director of operations described the culture in the early '90s as "complete cowboy management." He says, "I didn't have to talk to my boss about anything, because Michael was always in my office. It was ready, fire, aim. That worked where you had the right people." An operations manager who was hired in the '80s described this "no permission" culture and entrepreneurial approach in the early days. She said, "The entire North American materials planning team at the time was just a few people. The materials and production planning teams would get together every morning and figure out what parts we had on hand and what we could get hold of that morning. Then we'd figure out what we could build and tell the sales guys to go sell that. You just figured it out, and you never asked permission in the beginning." Even as the company grew in the '90s, the entrepreneurial spirit and speed remained. "When we did start to get some structure," she says, "there was so much trust between the bosses and the workers.

Approvals were fast."

This rapid-fire execution was highly data-driven, which created some guardrails or rules of engagement while allowing the company to pivot quickly (creative agility). Dell had an advantage in this area: because it sold direct, it had data about what its customers bought, how many times they called, what ads they responded to, and how often their machines broke. As Bill Sharpe, the former CEO of ad agency Sharpe Blackmore, says, "Dell was doing big data way before everyone else, and that was an advantage. We started building an analytical model with feeds from Dell's call center that tracked variables like spend, region, colour, ad placement, and the like, and then ran a regression that predicted the number of phone calls you'd get. This allowed us to quickly identify what was working and not, and constantly refine and redeploy the budget. We were at least ten years ahead of our time on Big Data. The critical thing was, it was highly, highly actionable. And the competition literally could not keep up."

In the early days, partners such as Bill Sharpe also noted the company's willingness to take risks (a shared value): "A lot of other clients go on autopilot – 'Let's run TV for 13 weeks and then get ready for spring season.' They are not out there actively saying 'What can we do to change things?' And so what happened was, Dell significantly unbalanced the competition. The competition was too legacy bound, too enterprise bound, and they had no analytics. All they started to do was follow what we were doing. IBM started running ads that looked virtually the same. So we wrote the president of IBM Canada a letter saying, 'You know what, we can save you a lot of money. Just have us do your ads, because we have all the templates, and your ads are so similar to ours. You won't have to pay your expensive agency.' We never got a response." Data-driven risk-taking allowed employees to be bold in their decision-making and nimble in response to competitors.

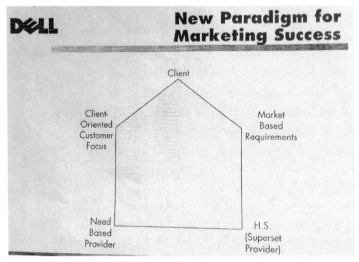

Figure 5.4. Tom Martin's presentation to the marketing group, April 1993.

One example of this risk-taking and resulting speed of execution was the company's handling of the Intel floating-point unit crisis of 1994. I was 31, and had just been promoted to marketing director for North American corporate desktops, Dell's largest product business. I had uncharacteristically decided to actually take the entire Thanksgiving holiday off. (Within about six months of my joining Dell, my workaholism – or commitment, depending on your point of view – was legendary. My boss, Tom Martin, jokingly showed this PowerPoint slide in a marketing meeting in April 1993, ostensibly to explain how projects would be resourced in our fifty-plus-person group – note the initials of the jack-of-all-trades "Superset Provider" in the lower right of Figure 5.4).

I'd driven three hours from Austin to Dallas to have dinner with a friend and was just sitting down to eat my turkey dinner when my phone rang. It was Tom, explaining that there was a crisis associated with Intel and that he needed me to come back to Austin that very day. *The New York Times* had just run an article detailing how the Pentium chip miscalculated very large numbers.[7] The flaw affected all of the millions of Pentium computers already shipped. Dell was the leader in Pentium chip shipments. It was the only time I'd ever heard Tom sound worried. Intel, a $10 billion company at the time, would eventually take a $475 million charge to earnings, the equivalent of half a year's R&D budget, as a result of the crisis.[8]

At 6 PM that evening I was in Tom's office in Austin. We spent four hours discussing a possible plan of attack. The next morning, about 15 Dell employees – including me, a director of operations, and Jeff Clarke (then director of desktop engineering and now vice-chairman of Dell) – met in a conference room. Whenever we were gathered in a room together, it usually meant something serious had hit the fan. The director of operations described why the three of us were in the room for most major crises of the '90s: "We shared a common trait: we could see the solution to a problem. 'Houston, we have a problem.' We didn't need to think about it for a long time. Just do it. Dell was lucky from that standpoint – it had people who could look at big problems, and say 'The solution is this and this – and if we execute to that, we'll be alright.' Dell let that talent rise."

The problem had found us. It was time to generate ideas, evaluate alternatives, and plan – at lightning speed. I grabbed a whiteboard marker and started scribbling ideas as people threw them out. About three hours later, we had figured out that the first step in solving the crisis was to educate customers. The Pentium chip error only affected those doing very complex calculations, such as extremely precise science and engineering applications.[9] The typical customer would never see it. Second, we would provide the customers who believed they were affected with a field-replaceable chip module. Those customers were likely to be technically sophisticated enough to replace the chip module themselves, which would save considerably on the cost of shipping whole units from the customer to Dell and back. Third, for customers unable to swap out the chipset themselves but still concerned about the impact of the error, we would ship the computer to a Dell facility, make the repair, and ship it back to customers.

With those decisions made, I suggested to the team that our top priority had to be running the numbers so that we could size the financial impact and put it in front of Mort Topfer, Dell's vice-chairman, for approval. At that point, some valuable creative abrasion occurred. An experienced manager (whom I did not yet know) raised his hand and politely but firmly said, "Excuse me, Heather. With all due respect, running the numbers to get Mort's approval is not our top priority. I have hundreds of tech support reps on the phones. And they are getting a thousand calls a day about this problem. They cannot just shit an answer. We have to tell them what to say." And thus was I introduced to the extremely colorful and usually correct director of technical support, Steve Smith, a two-time Purple Heart in Vietnam who looked out for his people and commanded the respect of all he led. Steve was right, and his direction would prove to be critical in Dell's handling of the crisis. Dell was one of the first to have a response for customers. Those customers were particularly panicked, since Intel insisted, right up until December 20, 1994,[10] that the flaw was minor and they would only replace chipsets, at their discretion, once they (Intel) had interviewed customers to determine if they actually needed such a replacement. This was even after IBM had deemed the problem serious enough that it halted all shipments of computers with Pentium-based processors on December 12, 1994.[10]

But the question was, what were we actually going to tell the call center reps to say? That would impact the financials, and vice versa. Fortunately, Kellie Leonard, a member of the public relations ("PR") team who looked so young I was sure she was an intern, volunteered to write the scripts and craft messages for the media. On day one, Kellie produced the simplest of messages, which was that Dell would take care of their customers, including replacing their chipsets if customers so desired. This message did a lot to calm frenzied customers, who weren't interested in Intel's description of the problem and simply wanted a correct chip in place of the flawed one they had. The only trouble with this message was a financial risk: Intel at the time had not committed any dollars to help manufacturers such as Dell fund the replacements. As far as we knew, Dell could be on the hook for the full repair.

The same day, I calculated the cost to Dell, debated whether we could afford to use the blanket statement "We will take care of our customers" with the PR team, and walked into Mort Topfer's office with the head of PR. I told him that based on my calculations, we could not afford to lead with the blanket statement that we would take care of customers. I said, "Mort, if we do that, the costs could be huge. We could go out of business." I started to explain the calculations on the spreadsheet I'd brought with me. Mort glanced for a moment at the spreadsheet, then looked up and said, "I'm sure these calculations are correct. And if we don't take care of our customers, we'll go out of business anyway." Decision made. As we were leaving, Mort called me back in to his office and added, "Heather, you know that number you showed me? I need you to get it down to about a tenth of that." Of course.

With Mort's quick go-ahead, we went with Kellie's script for the call center reps and avoided the PR issues that subsequently ensued for Intel. Our opening line, "We will take care of our customers," calmed customers' anxiety. They were then able to listen rationally to our description of the problem and who was likely to be affected by it. Most customers concluded it wasn't them. I walked the technical support floor the next day, and to a person, every rep was following Kellie's script exactly. Steve Smith was in the house.

Dell had assessed the Pentium chip problem, developed a technical solution, run the numbers, created communications scripts, trained support reps, and gotten approval for the plan, all before competitors returned from the Thanksgiving holiday. But we weren't done yet. Because Dell had very low inventory levels, it didn't have many systems with the flawed chips on hand. This created an opportunity to demonstrate the power of the direct model.

On the Friday before Christmas of that year, about ten Dell marketing leaders held a conference call. I was the only one still in Austin, as everyone else had left for vacation. Tom Martin asked me, "Heather, what do you think? Do we have the updated chips in all our product?" Earlier that day, I had spoken with a senior manufacturing director, who told me he was 95% sure they had gotten all of the flawed chips out of inventory, and the math associated with our low inventory levels certainly said that was likely. I relayed that to the team, and we decided to run an ad guaranteeing that we had the clean chips. The following full page ad ran in *The Wall Street Journal* ("WSJ") on January 4, 1995, and this is all it said:

Figure 5.5. Dell's ad in The Wall Street Journal, *January 4, 1995, from the author's collection.*

Rapid changes in the technology industry can result in crises that threaten industry leaders – but the same factors that create innovation can help manage those upsets. Dell's rapid decision-making and calculated risk-taking turned the Pentium chip flaw into a textbook example of PR crisis management, and a marketing coup. It demonstrated the advantages of Dell's model and its ability to execute at great speed despite its growing size. More importantly, it strengthened customer relationships

and enhanced Dell's reputation. And the plan had
not broken the bank: financial costs were about 10%
of what I had calculated, thanks largely to effective
customer communication.

A former human resources director sums it up: "A
lot of companies can commit to a strategy, but they
don't know how to execute it. Dell actually knew
how to execute what it put forward. A lot of people
put pretty plans in place, but they don't know how to
execute. Dell did."

Risk-taking was one of Dell's core shared values
in the '80s and '90s. Rapid-fire, data-driven decision-
making and a strong focus on execution helped create
creative agility in the face of numerous opportunities
and challenges.

The final factor in Dell's success in the '90s,
according to participants I interviewed, was
leadership, starting at the top. As one former manager
notes, "I hate those gross displays of power. And that
was something I appreciated about Michael Dell.
He was not a 'kiss my ring' kind of guy. He never
screamed at anyone." Michael was known for rolling
up his sleeves and for his informal conversations
with employees. An operations manager describes
her first meeting with Michael: "I was in a meeting,
and we were talking about hard drives. Suddenly,
this guy who looks like he's 15 starts reeling off the

specs of all the hard drives, the delivery times, and the prices. With no notes. I kept leaning further and further forward across the table, straining to see his nametag, wondering who this young genius was. Finally, I read it – Michael. At that point I realized that 'Michael' was the CEO of the company, and he was now looking at ME quizzically, wondering why I was staring at him."

A former corporate communications manager recalls Michael's focus on the details. She told me, "One day I answered my phone, and heard, 'Hi, this is Michael.' I said, 'Michael who?' There was a pause, and I said, 'You mean the Michael who signs my paychecks?' He said, 'That's the one.' He was calling to make sure I had taken out a line in a press release we had written."

A former marketing director recalls, "Michael was very accessible in the early days. He was in all our quarterly marketing meetings, and he knew my name, even though I was a very junior employee. We all felt very safe bringing up ideas and issues with him. Some of the other execs Dell brought in later, you didn't really want to run into them in the hall."

I had a similar experience myself in 2014, while writing this book. In November 2014, I attended Dell's conference for customers, Dell World, along with about 5,000 others. On the second day, I happened to be coming up an escalator when Michael was coming down, alone except for someone I presumed to be a PR person. It had been over ten years since I had seen Michael, so I politely greeted him, not expecting him to remember me. "Heather," he immediately replied, "great to see you here! Thanks for coming." Michael was as down-to-earth as ever. He rarely forgot the names of the "pioneers" who helped him build the company. Which is remarkable for someone who meets tens of thousands of people every year. There were very few "prima donna" executives at Dell in the early days, Michael included. This made them accessible and approachable, which fostered both the sharing of innovative ideas and the speed of decision-making and execution.

Michael was also known for his humor. The former operations director recalls his first meeting with Michael: "My first meeting with Michael, we're sitting in the ninth floor conference room. And he said anytime you have to run down to accounting to get a vendor paid and you're selling furniture out of the lobby, it's not looking good." (The former corporate communications manager also remembers those days, noting, "We were literally selling these really nice Herman Miller bookshelves and tables out the back door to raise cash in the early '90s.")

I experienced Michael's nerdy sense of humor myself, when I was working for Joel. Cary Davis, Michael's executive assistant at the time, and I were working on the presentation package for a board of directors meeting. Late one evening, I phoned Cary's office to discuss a problem I had found in one of the pie charts. A male voice answered, "Hello! Pete's Pizza. What can I get on your pie?" After a few seconds of stunned silence, I heard a paroxysm of schoolboy giggles, and then Cary came on the line.

"Cary, who the hell was that?" I asked.

He paused. "Ummm... that was Michael."

Right. Guess he wasn't as worked up about the board meeting as we were. Michael was fun to work with, even when he was posing some new, insane challenge with a completely straight face, like "I'd like to start measuring our inventory in hours, not days." Which, sure enough, we did.

Michael also cares about the people he works with. In May 2000, on my last day before I left on my first maternity leave, my assistant came around the corner of my cube, eyes as big as saucers. "Someone claiming to be Michael Dell is on the phone," she said. "Do you want to talk to him?" She put him through. Michael told me that he just wanted to wish me well with the pregnancy and he really hoped I'd come back to Dell at the end of my leave.

Figure 5.6. Author's Dell Internet Assessment certificate from 1998.

Michael can also see around corners – he is a visionary. In the mid-'90s, I was head of North American corporate desktop marketing – and was trying to grow a multi-billion-dollar product line, Dell's biggest in North America, at close to 50% year on year. During that time, Michael had identified the internet as a game-changing opportunity to extend the direct model. In the fall of 1994, Michael's executive assistant, Scott Eckert, absolutely would not stop bugging me to put my product specifications up on the internet. (It was on my list, but near the bottom). Dell was one of the first companies to have an intranet, an internet site, and eventually, e-commerce. So I asked team member Pamposh Zutshi to take care of getting our product specs on the website. Pamposh asked, "Heather, how much time should I spend on this? Is it important, or just a check-box exercise?" I said, "PZ, it's just a check-box. I don't think this internet thing's gonna take off." At the moment, I'm not confident this smart watch thing is going to take off, for those of you looking for investment ideas.

Michael has two other hidden talents that serve him well. First, as he has publicly said, he never thinks he's the smartest guy in the room. And if he does, he goes and finds another room. (Truth be told, the smartest guy in the room at Dell in the early days was often probably my old boss Tom Martin, the VP of Marketing – but he was smart enough to know that this talent did not extend to the execution of his ideas.) Michael's humility in this regard keeps him listening carefully to, and learning from, many others (including customers). Second, he has a remarkable ability to see connections between disparate ideas to create value for customers, as noted by Clayton Christensen in his insightful 2011 book, *The Innovator's DNA*. Christensen compared leading CEOs such as eBay's Pierre Omidyar, Intuit's Scott Cook, RIM's Michael Lazaridis, Michael Dell, and 5,000 others on five discovery skills known to foster innovative thinking. Michael Dell scored in the ninetieth percentile on four of the five – associating, questioning, experimenting, and networking.[11]

Michael also famously aligned the entire Dell team around common objectives and encouraged the shared value of commitment by giving all employees stock options, creating hundreds of accidental "Dellionaires" in the process. (Employees hired in the chaotic and often crisis-filled '80s and early '90s could not have predicted this outcome.) The wealth effect was incredible, with thirty-somethings building 8,000-square-foot houses on Lake Austin. In the process, he also transformed Austin from a mid-sized town full of students, aging hippies, and government employees (unofficial town motto, as seen today on colorful tie-dye t-shirts: "Keep Austin Weird") to a high-tech mecca of 2 million people.

And Dell's smart, connected, and committed leadership extended well beyond Michael Dell. As former marketing director Indraj Gill put it, "I used to go to Tom's office for a price move, and after an hour I'd be spent. Tom Martin was one of the top five reasons we succeeded. He was so smart. Mort, Tom Meredith (former CFO), Michael, Joel were also key." There were other well-respected leaders who valued risk-taking and execution, including then-product engineering director (and now vice-chairman) Jeff Clarke. A former manager notes, "Jeff was hell on wheels, and he was a pied piper. He was all about execution, but he also cared deeply about the people, the products, and the company. He was bright, caring, and articulate. He had a phrase, 'Not execution. Flawless execution.'"

In Dell's early years, accessible leadership helped speed decision-making and execution, key shared values in its early culture. The lack of hierarchy minimized guardrails or rules of engagement and prevented employees from getting bogged down in bureaucracy.

"What we didn't have was a view as to, 'what is a game-changer that could kill us?'"

—Tom Martin, former VP marketing

TA DA.

you can save the time and expense of multiple POs by ordering your system and software with just one purchase order to Dell.

That's right. You'll get all of this from Dell. The $2 billion Dell. The FORTUNE 500® Dell. The third largest PC manufacturer in the entire world, Dell. And now the we'll-load-all-the-applications-that-you-want-for-just-$15 Dell.

And get prepared blow away the compet notes on your desk.

SIX

Culture Shift

DELL'S BUSINESS MODEL ADVANTAGE AND risk-taker's culture was the stuff of business school legend. But, during the period from roughly 2001 to 2012, it became a double-edged sword. Because of the focus on improving on the direct business model, the Dell team did not spend enough time on creative abrasion and creative resolution – encouraging and debating new ideas, then being patient enough to hold those ideas in creative tension rather than simply picking between one suboptimal option or another. The former operations director put it simply: "We were so good at execution, we didn't have as much time for innovation." Tom Martin also believes that Dell's focus on execution had an effect on its ability to innovate as it became a bigger company. He says, "From 1990 to 1993, we spent the time to understand that the business model was our advantage, the asset we had. Then we worked very hard to come up with the executional approach that was consistent with that advantage. The culture you build to focus on executing on a decades-long advantage turns out to probably be inimical to innovation. So you have an asset, you work to create tens of thousands of people who are good at executing on that advantage. And then that advantage goes away. So now you have a culture that is good at executing on a cost advantage. But that culture is not very good at changing the game. What we didn't have was a view to 'what is a game changer that could kill us?' We really didn't have conversations about that. And there was an element of the culture that actively looked down its nose at the conversation about 'could there be a major shift that would really change things?'" During the period Tom describes, employees focused their efforts on executing on the company's existing advantage: the direct model.

The former operations director also believes that Dell should have debated whether changes to its business model were required earlier in the game: "In the '90s, Scott Flaig [SVP operations] pulled all 2,000 people in operations together and said, we're a distributor. Lots of people looked at him funny, because they thought we were a manufacturer. But if you switch to thinking about being a distributor, then it really doesn't matter where you build it. I do think maybe we took that a bit too far – which is why at

$60 billion this is a tougher company to run. Direct became ubiquitous when the internet came on – there were much lower barriers to entry. Amazon has done the direct model well. You shop there because you can get anything there, delivered when they say. And you totally trust them." The operations director continues, "We were so narrowly focused on the distribution model – we applied it to servers, to workstations. We did not spend enough time on the think-tank level. This model has a bottom to it. First, the industry consolidated. Then, the low-cost Asian manufacturers jumped in – Acer, Lenovo. Then the South Koreans – Samsung. And the South Koreans have always been good at distribution."

The relentless reliance on the business model in the mid-2000s dampened innovation in other areas. A former marketing director says, "Another executive told me how he'd propose something and be told, 'No, stick to the model. Don't deviate from the model.' What kind of empowerment was that? It drove out innovation." Dell's over-reliance on its business model and its pace of execution reduced creative abrasion and prevented creative resolution.

During the 2000s, Dell's leadership also shifted. Asked what the #1 factor was in Dell's decline beginning in the mid-2000s, a former human resources director said, "Michael Dell pulled himself out of the day-to-day operations. He thought he had enough players in place, but you had people who didn't really care about Dell. He stepped out. That was probably the biggest factor."

Executive succession is common, healthy, and, at some point, inevitable. However, in the mid-2000s, Dell's leadership changes were also accompanied by changes in culture and shared values as employee headcount nearly doubled, from 46,000 to 91,500, in three years. These new employees brought in a very different problem-solving approach, different shared values, and new processes and rules of engagement. The conflict between these new employees and the entrepreneurial types who drove Dell's first two decades, coupled with the shift in leadership, significantly changed the company's culture and appetite for risk-taking. Instead of creative abrasion, we had cost reduction, process optimization, and restructuring.

Michael has always brought in people with divergent skill sets to help him. For example, from 1986 to 1990, venture capitalist Lee Walker served as president. Former Motorola executive Mort Topfer was vice-chairman of Dell from 1994 to 1999. These other leaders brought skills that were complementary to Michael's vision and marketing talent. But Michael was always co-CEO or part of the "office of the CEO," providing a crucial link to Dell's entrepreneurial shared values of risk-taking, speed, and execution.

In July 2004, Dell elevated former Bain consultant Kevin Rollins to sole CEO, and Michael Dell became chairman. Rollins had joined Dell in 1996, when Dell's sales were about $5 billion, and became president of Dell Americas later that year. Rollins and Michael Dell shared a glass-partitioned office until Rollins resigned in January 2007 (when Dell revenues were over $55 billion). Results from this period are shown in Figure 6.1 ("CAGR" refers to compound annual growth rate), with adjacent periods for comparison.

	1991-2003	2003-2006	2006-2012*
Dell Revenue CAGR	37.7%	11.6%	-.1%
Dell Net Income CAGR	38.9%	-.5%	-1.4%
PC Industry Unit CAGR	16.0%	14.4%	7.3%
Dell Unit CAGR	41.2%	14.8%	-.2%
Dell Multiple of Industry Growth	2.6X	1.0X	NM**
End of Period Market Share	16.9%	17.1%	11.1%
End of Period Employees	46,000	91,500	111,300

Figure 6.1. Key Dell metrics over three time periods.

Note, Figure 6.1: Dell's fiscal year end is January 31. Therefore, the Dell data for revenues, net income, and employees for "2003-2006" represents the period from January 31, 2004 through January 31, 2007, and so on. All other figures are as of December 31 of the noted year.[1,2,3,4]

* Dell went private in October 2013. Therefore, 2012 is the last full year for which results are available.

** Not meaningful. Dell's unit growth was slightly negative during this period, against a PC industry growth of about 7%.

By the mid-2000s, the personal computer industry was becoming a tougher place to operate in, especially for Dell. Growth had begun to slow, except in Asia, where the direct model had less traction. PC prices and margins also declined as low-cost Asian manufacturers entered the industry and the industry consolidated (HP bought Compaq in 2001, Lenovo bought IBM's PC business in 2004, and Acer bought Gateway in 2007). Asian manufacturers had labour costs that were about 80% lower than costs in the US and Europe.[5] In addition, the growth of smaller, less configurable mobile devices meant that Dell's build-to-order model had less value for consumers and corporations. Finally, the driver of innovation and growth shifted from the corporation to the consumer

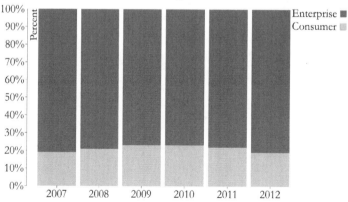

Figure 6.2. Dell's mix of consumer vs. enterprise revenues. For this chart, "enterprise" refers to business, government, and education accounts.[1]

(a phenomenon known as the "consumerization of IT" and exemplified by the ubiquity and utility of personal smartphones). As shown in Figure 6.2, the consumer segment represented less than 20% of Dell's sales. This shift to the consumer also led to a greater focus on intuitive, elegant design, which was not Dell's strength.

It was a tough hand to play. PC industry growth rates continued to drop as more smartphones and tablets were introduced. However, Dell's growth slowed even more dramatically during the period 2003 to 2006, dropping from 2.6X the industry growth rate to 1X the industry growth rate. In 2007, HP surpassed Dell as the PC industry unit market share leader. Dell's revenue and net income growth also slowed significantly, and Dell repeatedly missed analysts' earnings expectations. Other metrics suffered as well. A drive to cut costs by staffing US call centers with temporary employees led to a decline in Dell's US consumer customer satisfaction ratings from 79 (in 2004) to 74 (in 2005), the steepest decline in the industry.[6] In 2006, Dell recalled 4.1 million laptops with defective Sony-made batteries, but not before internet videos of flaming laptops made Dell a reluctant internet sensation.[7] Some criticized Dell for being slow to offer faster and cheaper AMD processors (chips) in addition to Intel chips.[7] These

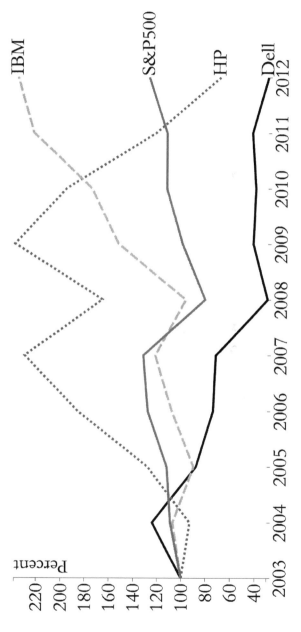

Figure 6.3. Stock price by competitor. All data are as of December 31 of the noted year.[8]

factors influenced Dell's stock price relative to competitors, as shown in Figure 6.3 (the stock price at December 31, 2003, is used as the base price and set to 100% for all competitors).

As we will see later, the drop in stock price intensified pressure on Dell to achieve earnings targets and reduced experimentation at the company.

THE CONSULTANT(S) IN THE NEXT CUBE

During this time, Rollins was instrumental in helping Dell put in place the infrastructure required of a mature $50 billion company. A former corporate communications manager notes, "Before Kevin got there, we were always rounding the corner on three wheels at 100 miles an hour. He made sure we hired enough people that the wheels did not fall off." As noted in Figure 6.1, Dell almost doubled its employee count between the end of 2003 and the end of 2006, from 46,000 to 91,500. Many ex-consultants from Bain, McKinsey, and other shops were hired during this period. By the time I returned to Austin in 1999, following a two-year assignment in Toronto, it seemed like you couldn't swing a slinky without hitting a former consultant. They were everywhere, and they brought a significantly different perspective than the entrepreneurial types who drove Dell's first two decades.

The influx of Ivy League-educated, highly analytical consultants helped Dell think about strategy, not just execution. "That was a good thing Michael did – bringing Bain in – they brought visionary talent. We were so focused on execution – we needed another layer to define what the strategy was. Kevin Rollins, for example, got us out of retail – because of the channel conflict," noted a former operations director. The former consultants also developed some of the analytical models that capitalized on Dell's advantage in having direct data about the customer.

But the consultants also brought a strong process orientation, a focus on cost-cutting, and a seemingly endless quest for data that was antithetical to Dell's "risk-taker's" mentality. In addition, the consultants brought a very consistent background and rigorous approach to solving problems (in contrast to the fast-moving implementers populating the company at the time). I worked at consulting company McKinsey & Co. from 1990 to 1992, with some of the smartest people I've ever met (a few with arrogance to match). At McKinsey and other consulting firms, the quest for the "right answer" is paramount; it's pursued with relentless vigor and, sometimes, a degree of intellectual arrogance. As McKinsey partner Pete

Walker noted in a 1993 *Fortune* article, "It's almost
never that we fail because we come up with the
wrong answer. We fail because we don't properly
bring along management. And if the company just
doesn't have the horses, there are limits to what we
can do."[9] Oh my.

A former executive describes the impact of the
consultants' quest for more data as follows: "I think a
large part of it is: up until Dell hit about $25 billion,
it was driven by a bunch of executives with the 90s
mindset – just get out there and get it done. No
excuses. The leadership celebrated quick decisions
made with imperfect data. The mantra was: 'Get it
done, learn quickly, adjust.' Then, by the early 2000s,
Dell recruited a large number of senior executives,
many of whom were former consultants. Some of
them were like former 777 pilots – very used to
sophisticated instruments. So we brought them in
and put them in what must have felt like a really
fast Cessna ... with an altimeter. As the plane starts
diving toward the ground, these guys are screaming,
'Where are my instruments? I need my instruments!'
Meanwhile, the simple altimeter clearly tells them
they are nose-diving and should pull up on the stick.
In the 2000s, it was all about the quest for the perfect
data."

Typical McKinsey studies, predicated on an exhaustive data-gathering and problem-solving approach, could last 2 to 12 months. This works in some industries but not in high tech, where Moore's Law rules. Wait 6 months to make a decision, and you could miss most of a product cycle.

Bill Sharpe, head of Dell Canada's former ad agency, notes, "Dell had a split personality back in the mid 1990s. It was, on one hand, a profoundly sales-driven culture – lots of hyper sales guys. But there were always consultants, also, throughout the time I worked with Dell. Ex-McKinsey, Ex-Bain, etc., etc. Consultants who tended to think a lot and didn't do much. There were more consultants over time. And consultants who moved into marketing who never should have been there. I had a Dell marketing guy [we'll call him John] who was a former consultant come to me years after we'd worked together. John told me, 'I was uninformed about marketing. Marketing always has to push forward, to go. Whereas I was always saying no, stop, prove it to me.'" Sharpe continues, "This, to me, was the timeframe when Dell lost its way. That's not the way marketing works. You have to test, refine, go." Indeed, Roger Martin, the business school dean and a former consultant himself, says that the two words that will kill innovation are "prove it." Martin suggests:

There is no data about how a genuinely new idea will interact with the world in advance of said new idea actually interacting with the world. Therefore there is no way to prove it will work in advance.[10]

CULTURE SHIFT AND BUREAUCRACY

A former human resources director describes the impact of the massive influx of consultants on Dell's culture: "During 1999, we were bringing on thousands of people. Dell knew it was having difficulties acculturating the new people. Dell had to teach them and say, 'Everyone has a plan, but very few people can execute it.' It had a 50% turnover of director and VP levels in the first six months. In the first six months, most high fliers from other companies failed. If you were a people manager, you had to be a 5,000 foot/50,000 foot people manager. One day, you had to have the details, then the next day you had to be able to talk strategy at the highest levels. There are very few people who are wired to be 'strategic doers.' They're either one or the other." Finding a critical mass of these strategic doers was not easy, but Dell managed to do it through the early 2000s by looking specifically for such attributes as "dealing with ambiguity" and "learning on the fly" when hiring. And then Dell began its massive hiring effort in 2004, adding 45,000 employees in a few short years.

The human resources director continues: "Dell realized [in the early 2000s] it had the wrong hiring model, because it kept hiring these people who were very, very strategic, and couldn't get in and do the work. Dell had MBA students by the hundreds coming in. It lost its culture. It lost its ways. After a while, Dell had as many cultures as they had managers, because each one was interpreting it a different way. When Dell came out with the Soul of Dell, it was trying to get back to that, that culture, but employees didn't have the person sitting in front of them, saying this is what I believe, this is the direction that we should be going."

The sheer number of new employees from 2004 to 2006 also drove the development of that dreaded big-company disease – bureaucracy. In February 2007, when Dell's board asked him to return as the company's CEO, Michael Dell wrote the following in an internal memo to Dell employees:

> We have great people ... but we also have a new enemy, bureaucracy, which costs us money and slows us down. We created it, we subjected our people to it, and we have to fix it![11]

I experienced the increase in bureaucracy myself over time. This is best illustrated by two contrasting stories. A couple of months after joining Dell in 1992, I was speaking with an engineer, the late Dennis Burleson, about a product he was offering in "stealth mode" to one of our largest customers. The product he described to me was preinstalled software – software that came "ready to run" when you fired up your PC. This was back in the early '90s, when computers came with a blue or black screen, the operating system installed, and not much else. Installing application software such as Microsoft Office meant sitting at your desk with a cup of coffee, a stack of at least three 5¼" floppy diskettes for installation, and a couple of hours to spare. Dennis explained that he had written a software script that loaded the application software ordered by the customer onto the hard drive as it made its way down Dell's assembly line. Because Dell built computers to the customer's specific order, it could, using Dennis's script, load the customer's required software for them. Other competitors, who built standard computers for resellers' inventory, would have no idea what software to put on each PC. They instead relied on resellers to do this at the point of sale. Dennis's idea was simple, brilliant, met a significant customer need, and was something only Dell could do. I asked, "Dennis, how many people have you told about this idea?" Not many. Dennis replied that he did not have enough resources as it was and said, "If we told the world about this, I'd be swamped." Exactly. Dennis agreed that if I could triple his resources, he would let me tell the world about the idea.

I raced back to my desk, ballparked the economics of the idea for Dell, and wrote an email directly to Dell's president, Joel Kocher, proposing that we launch the business and triple Dennis's resources. I had only been at Dell two months and had never met Joel, so I thought that he might not read my email. In 45 minutes, he sent me a note back: "Sounds good. You need a sales comp [compensation] plan. Go." Six months later, with a rookie brand manager at the helm and a lot of help from colleagues such as Tricia Traeger, Bob Gutermuth, Jenny Adkins, and Dennis Burleson, we launched ReadyWare: 81 software titles that could be preinstalled to any Dell customer's order. (It was supposed to be 82 titles, but Reader Rabbit Math was somehow misplaced.) It was a brand new business for Dell, led by a rookie with no formal authority or resources and launched in six months during the early '90s.

Figure 6.4. *ReadyWare ad circa 1993, from the author's collection.*

Fast forward to May 2003, when I was director of marketing for Dell Canada. My boss (a former Bain consultant), told me that within the next three months we needed to dramatically reduce sales costs by shifting about half of Dell Canada's consumer sales force to Hyderabad, India. Setting up a call center in India had been done before, in the US and a few other geographies, as well as by Dell Canada's technical support team. Dell Canada's own financial services team had just begun the process. Dell had a call center building in Hyderabad, with empty seats waiting to be staffed. My boss (we'll call him Tim) gave me the contact information for a Dell group in the US (we'll call the group Global Call Centers) managing the process and assisting regions that wanted to shift headcount to lower-cost geographies. I phoned the lead for this group, who explained that it would take 12 to 18 months to make the transition to Hyderabad. I was incredulous. What were we doing? Developing a skyscraper? Building a rocket ship? Brokering peace between warring nations? What on earth took so long? I asked as much, and he told me it would take at least six weeks to fill out their form. "Then it goes into the queue and we review it," he said. "Then we might have some questions. There are lots of other regions trying to do this too, you know, and we are managing the process for all of them." I interrupted, "You'll have your form in two days. And I'll wait a week for you to get back to me with a date by which we can meet your rep in Hyderabad. If you don't get back to me by then, we'll do it ourselves." I think he thought I was kidding.

We submitted the form two days later, putting our best estimates in for complex questions, such as the proportion of calls we thought could be handled by our Canadian reps vs. our future Hyderabad call center. I let the Global Call Centers lead know the form was in and politely waited the interminable week (patience is not one of my virtues). At the end of May 2003, I phoned our best and most senior sales manager, Tara Fine, a 28-year-old woman with great leadership skills. Tara's outstanding interpersonal skills belied a steely resolve and "whatever it takes" attitude. And she had sales chops; her single-day record for sales by an inside sales rep still stands today. I offered Tara the opportunity to build Dell Canada's sales organization in India as a three-to-six-month project. (Even I thought three months was a bit tight given that India was halfway around the globe and neither one of us had ever been there.) Tara asked to think about it for a day. About two weeks later, Tara was on her way to the airport for her flight to India.

That very day, my boss, Tim, called me. He was concerned that Tara, with only six years of working solely in Canada under her belt, might not have the experience to handle the complexity of this start-up effort in a foreign country. Thinking that sending someone else might be a better choice, he asked, "Do you have a back-up plan?" I replied, "Tim, no, I don't have a back-up plan. Tara's our very best sales leader, and she's started new businesses for Dell before. She'll find a way to get it done. And if you really want me to develop a back-up plan, you better tell me now. Because she's on her way to the airport as we speak."

Tara landed in India, hired an outstanding senior sales manager to run operations there, and within the next few weeks had hired 42 sales representatives and four sales managers. She also addressed numerous operational issues, not the least of which was balancing call volumes so that they flowed between India and Canada appropriately given the resources available in each call center at various times during the day. (OK, so the Global Call Centers team might have been right about that one – it was a complex question requiring considerable analysis.) On August 18, 2003, we took our first call in Hyderabad. We'd pulled the whole thing off ourselves in just over three months, including the two weeks I spent impatiently "following" the corporate process and waiting for it to work. Within a year, those Hyderabad reps were hitting the same performance targets as our Toronto reps. Back in Canada, I had managed to not screw up the sales organization too badly, thanks to two of our sales managers who stepped up considerably to help me.

The Global Call Centers team had not completely forgotten us. About two weeks before Tara's team took our first call in Hyderabad, I got a call from a Global Call Centers representative. She said that she had reviewed our form and had a few questions. No wonder the damn process typically took 12 to 18 months! Launching a brand new, industry-first business from scratch with no formal resources took 6 months during the fast-moving '90s. Setting up a sales call center in India, following a known process previously executed by the US and your own technical support organization, and with "help" from a corporate team, was *planned* to take 12 to 18 months during the 2000s. Michael was right – bureaucracy was the new enemy.

The lesson? Through its hiring model, which looked specifically for the ability to deal with uncertainty and learn on the fly, Dell found a critical mass of "strategic doers," and this was a key part of its success through the early 2000s. And then, as it matured, Dell sought to bring in more strategists and build the infrastructure required of a mature company. This was likely a reasonable response to becoming a $50 billion company, but the shift in hiring was too much, too fast. The rapid growth in headcount and the influx of strategists, with their focus on intellectual rigor and process, dampened Dell's shared values of risk-taking and speed and created bureaucracies. This, in turn, reduced Dell's creative agility and ability to innovate.

RISK AVERSION

As noted above, one of the most significant aspects of the change in culture was a decline in risk-taking, which impacted the company's ability to innovate. A former executive says, "I think by the 2000s we had become a big company, more process-oriented, for the right reasons, because the dollars were so much bigger. But we might have taken it too far, too fast, and inadvertently discouraged risk-taking."

The company's success and related competition for resources may have been a factor. Marketing director Indraj Gill comments, "The risk-taking completely stopped. It changed from a meritocracy at some point ... When I was running Optiplex [corporate desktops], it took me two years to convince everyone we needed to split our product line. This was unpopular, because it meant we needed more resources we didn't have." Bill Sharpe adds, "I felt that the longer I worked with the company, the more risk averse it became, to the point I had to switch out the people who worked on it. The penchant for action is one of the things that actually slowed down in the company. What drove the risk aversion? It was so successful that, over time, nobody wanted to mess with the formula. Everybody thought the train would keep on rolling. What's the line – the emperor has no clothes? It was sacrilege to suggest that things might change. The tolerance for risk-taking in the company was, at the end, almost completely and totally, none."

Sharpe also saw the impact of the drive to execute on innovation. "I think it was entrepreneurial at the top, and at a certain managerial level. But below that, it was execution, execution, execution. Nobody was coming up with smart ideas. At Dell, what I saw was that, over time, innovation slowly got throttled down. I remember getting so many grey Dell Latitudes – my IT guy came in with a new Dell one day. And I remember thinking, OK, this is just like buying another Ford sedan. I wasn't going to take it home and show anyone."

Sharpe continues, "When we were doing a competitive review one day, I said, I think we better put Apple back in. After Jobs came back. Everyone laughed and said that's an idiotic idea. But I said, no, Jobs is capable of radical innovation."

Some Dell employees recognized the need to return to an innovative culture but were hampered by the fact that almost 80% of Dell's revenue was in commodity PC products, with low margins that did not permit significant investment in R&D. According to its annual reports, by the second quarter of Dell's fiscal year 2014 (the last quarter before it went private), Dell's R&D had climbed to 2.2% of revenue,[1] up from 1.2% in the fiscal year ended January 30, 2004. However, the 2014 figure was significantly less than that of rivals IBM, whose R&D totaled 6.2% of revenues for the closest equivalent period, and HP, whose R&D totaled 3.1% of revenues.[1] The more consumer-focused Apple

spent 3.3% of its 2014 sales on R&D.[1] A corporate
services director said, "At Dell, you had a dichotomy:
engineers who desperately wanted to go back to an
innovative culture, back to the days when PCs blew
up in the lab because you tried something new. But
they were also realists, who understood that PCs
were a commodity. On the other hand, they were also
looking at Apple in the early 2000s and saying these
guys are really innovative, and if we don't get back to
that, we'll be less than they are. And they were right."

Tom Martin gets the last word on the topic: "I
would say we had an anti-innovation culture. The
adoption of the belief in execution as the core took on
a quasi-religious cast, such that anything that didn't
look like that was viewed with suspicion." The death
of risk-taking (a shared value) at Dell, coupled with
a focus on executing on the core business and model,
eventually drove out creative abrasion as employees
stopped bringing new ideas forward. And the absence
of creative abrasion made creative resolution, so
critical to disruptive innovation, "not applicable."

PRESSURES OF WALL STREET

The pressure to hit Wall Street's earnings targets also
reduced Dell's ability to innovate. As Tom Martin
puts it, "Another damaging thing was the focus on

the stock price – all that execution was driving up the stock price. We had a formal proposal on mobile devices in 1998. It wasn't dismissed because it was too early but because it wouldn't materially add to the stock price. We thought it would be a $1 billion business within three years, and that was not enough. A couple years later, we would have projected a $5 billion business, but it would have cost real money to pursue it. So it would have been rejected because, by then, we were struggling to hit flat earnings."

He continues, "By the 2000s, the stock price did a lateral for ten years. At that time, conversations would be about Wall Street not understanding if we put money in X, and it knocked money off the stock price. 10% of it was about the intellectual component: having a group that can help you see what direction to take, and 90% was about managing Wall Street. Ideas would get rejected, either because they were immaterial or too big and would cost too much to go after. I hate to be so simple-minded about it, but I think that was most of the deal." Of course, many companies face the pressures of Wall Street. There were 5,008 companies listed on major US stock exchanges in 2013.[12] They all face these pressures. However, the pressure was accentuated for Dell, first, due to the company's extraordinary success. Dell's stock rose 19,008% between the end of 1991 and the end of 1999,[13] compared to a 91% increase for Apple's stock over the same period.[14] The stock market's expectations for Dell were very high. Second, a management shift and a related focus on cost-cutting increased pressure to "focus on the core" rather than experiment. Third, a market shift away from Dell's strengths (such as the explosion of consumer-driven innovation exemplified by Apple's "i" products) made achievement of targets difficult. And fourth, thin margins in commodity products left little room for error.

A 2012 study by Daniel Ferreira, Gustavo Manso, and Andre Silva concluded that the pressures of Wall Street impact a firm's ability to invest for the longer term:

> Public firms choose more conventional projects. Their managers appear shortsighted: they care too much about current earnings. They find it difficult to pursue complex projects that the market does not appear to understand well. Public firms go private after adverse shocks, when it is clear that their business models are no longer working, and there is a need for restructuring.[15]

Martin adds, "I remember parking lot conversations about mobile. When you go from a low percentage of laptops to a high percentage of laptops, you have a less configurable machine being built by the same outsourced company. So HP and Dell have the same supply chain, because they were outsourcing to the same guy. And then you could see that smaller devices were coming, which were even less configurable. This was 1998-1999. We had parking lot conversations about the mobile business and also formal business presentations. The conversation about treating this business as innovation-driven was treated like talking about transfer payments at the Republican convention – it wasn't done."

A former executive relates another story about the impact of being a public company on business decisions: "In the early 2000s we were tossing around some 'new' ideas in the product group. One such idea was digital [flat screen] TVs. We already had a big share of the world's flat panel displays and, with innovative execution, many believed that this 'adjacency' could be a multi-billion dollar business for Dell. With already stretched resources in marketing, procurement, and engineering, we took our first TV from PowerPoint to product in a few months. And we generated media attention and won awards at the CES [Consumer Electronics Show] tradeshow that year. But the big play was not consumer-oriented – businesses were on the cusp of a digital signage revolution. We had the relationships – we weren't going in cold. The beauty was we would not have to fight to get into these accounts. We already had a commanding share in desktops and notebooks, and we were getting there in servers and storage. It was the same account executive! This was 2004."

He continues, "We already had some revenue in digital TVs. We even had pilots lined up at some very large retailers. We needed a small investment to get serious. Unfortunately, in 2004-2005, Dell missed quarterly earnings a couple of times, which impacted the stock. So, the message was 'go back to the core.' We decided to pass on the opportunity. The rest is history."

This "focus on the core" in order to hit short-term earnings targets took its toll on Dell's ability to capitalize on major industry product transitions. Sharpe states, "Dell completely and totally failed to see where the future of personal computing was going – Apple moved into content, started to create an ecosystem. Dell missed content, ease of use, ease of design, the consumer, and perhaps most importantly, Dell missed mobile. At the end of 2006, Intel, Dell, and Microsoft all missed mobile – a huge tech transition and they missed it. All are still playing catch-up. MS buys Nokia, writes it off. Google buys Motorola, sells it for a vast loss. All these guys didn't see it coming."

Dell also struggled to find an inspiring purpose, an element in Hill's framework, after it achieved the #1 worldwide market share position in 2001. A former marketing director says, "Dell became a soul-sucking experience over time. It had a purpose at the beginning: to be #1. After we hit #1, it was 'then what?' There was nothing to strive for anymore. Dell had a purpose, but the purpose wasn't reset. It just became about cost-cutting: 'How can we squeeze more blood out of the turnip?' Employees became cogs in the machine."

Cost-cutting also impacted Dell's relationships with suppliers and partners. A former corporate communications manager recalls, "We were squeezing contractors and suppliers. We'd pay them in 45 to 60 days, instead of 30 days like most businesses. It was brutal." Bill Sharpe notes that Dell could be a difficult culture to partner with: "We had to put tough people on the account. Dell was an odd culture, in that, with few exceptions, it was not a particularly friendly or approachable culture. The demands on everyone were so intense, it took away the ability to create relationships or kick around ideas. You were kind of in a machine. Dell was kind of soulless. I called it Texas capitalism." As we will see in the next chapter, partnering with other companies, particularly start-ups, is vital to Dell's success moving forward.

The relentless focus on cost-cutting also took its toll on Dell's customer service. Ironically, Dell's stated mission was and is: "Dell's mission is to be the most successful computer company in the world at delivering the best customer experience in markets we serve." Bill Sharpe says, "Customer experience was terrible. Then the outsourcing of service went to India. I remember being on those calls – it was obvious it was not going well ... That's where Dell Hell started – a complete and total collapse of customer service and the outsourcing of everything – a hollowing out of what had worked. It was all part of this relentless cost reduction: reduce costs, reduce costs, reduce costs."

Some cost reduction was necessary because Dell's industry was commoditizing. However, the relentless focus on cost-cutting caused Dell to lose sight of its purpose and damaged Dell's reputation for service.

Deteriorating customer service. The pressures of Wall Street. A major cultural shift and the growth of bureaucracy. A decline in risk-taking and loss of purpose. Missed product transitions. A shift in the basis of competition (mobility and design) and in geographic growth engines. A narrow focus on cost-cutting and the model that had worked for so many years.

It was a hurricane of change, and Dell was not in the eye of the storm. Something had to be done. (Re-)enter the founder.

"Knowing that an asteroid is going to hit the earth is not really useful if you are not planning to launch missiles to knock it out of the sky. You have to work massively overtime on the belief that innovation or massive change is going to happen."

—Tom Martin, former VP of marketing

SEVEN

Reinvention

IN FEBRUARY 2007, MICHAEL DELL returned to the helm of the company he founded in his dorm room. After six years of effort and a vicious battle with corporate raider Carl Icahn, Dell went private in October 2013. The company now stands poised to begin a new chapter. I asked former employees what their vision of Dell's preferred future state would be. Getting a purpose back and restoring the entrepreneurial culture were high priorities.

Indraj Gill recommends, "Create a set of values that this company is about. Dell's gotta find what its purpose is. What kind of culture is valued? And then protect those people, even if they piss people off. Not caustic people but people who are doing the right thing for the business, not for personal gain. If the culture's about risk-taking, don't beat people up who make mistakes. Protect people who live the values. The risk-taking culture doesn't survive without leaders backing you up."

A former manager in corporate services believes revamped leadership is critical. She says, "To get Dell out of where it is and to go forward, it still needs leadership and employee commitment. I don't know if Dell can get the culture back. It is so big and has been there for so long now. If it did some really interesting recruiting, took risks at the leadership level, maybe. Hire mavericks, risk-takers, people who are not afraid to lead, with some charisma."

Those to-be-hired risk-takers need leaders who will listen. Tom Martin cites the military as an example of an efficient execution culture that encourages input from the front lines. He says, "It takes a special general to listen to the corporals who actually talk back to them – 'You know if you do that, we're going to be dead?' Michael is an extremely good listener. Any entity the size of Dell has people capable of solving these problems. He needs to make it clear to his lieutenants that they need to listen to these corporals who talk back. Michael was such a good listener, he may have made the fairly common mistake that everyone was like that and would listen. Dell executives needed to find the dissident players and bring them forward. And I'm not sure that happened."

Martin also suggests that some foresight and experimentation, as well as methods for investing capital in smaller firms, are critical. He says, "You do actually have to know what to do once you free yourselves from the stock market shackles. You need 5 or 10% of the population focused on figuring out what the game changers are. It would be easy enough to have a group of people focused on that. Whether you paid attention to them or not is a different thing. Knowing that an asteroid is going to hit the earth is not really useful if you are not planning to launch missiles to knock it out of the sky. You have to work massively overtime on the belief that innovation or massive change is going to happen. And as a management team, you've got to be willing to respond, and you have to be willing to do the experiments to address the change that's coming."

Martin also recommends that senior Dell executives take a venture capitalist's perspective on investment in new areas. He says, "Some simple projects can be launched with existing human resources and minimal capital, like ReadyWare. But at the other end of the spectrum, imagine that automotive computing were some day going to be a $50 billion business divided between three players. Someone at Dell has done the analysis and figured out that this is a game changer – but it's complicated. That's because the regulatory, legal and reliability environment of automotive requires prototypes and lobbying and testing. We need $10 million and thirty people to create a new venture. But the essence of that new venture is a PC, in a different form factor. So we need partners and standards, but it is in or near our wheelhouse. Now in this case I think our VCs [Dell's senior executives] need to make a different and difficult set of decisions. Such as, is it a decent business, on paper? Do we have the right people to experiment with this thing and are we willing to give them up to go do it? And how do we measure it?"

Indeed, Dell has to place some intelligent bets on technologies and companies in this age of exponential digital acceleration and disruption. I think Dell has to become an "Intelligent Gambler," using the framework (I may have spent too long in academia) in Figure 7.1.

In the Intelligent Gambler© framework, a company makes investments in a portfolio of new technologies based on the risk associated with the degree of difference between the current business and the new business, and also the capital required to launch the new business. The required rate of return (the "hurdle rate") rises as the degree of difference increases (to the right on the horizontal axis) and as the degree of complexity rises (up on the vertical axis). For example, some projects are relatively similar to the current business (in this case, PCs) and require only

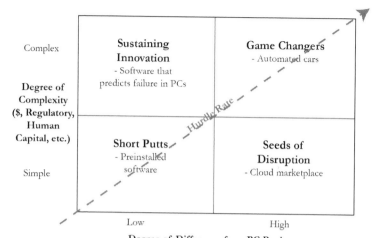

Figure 7.1. *Intelligent Gambler© framework for managing corporate venture investments.*

existing human resources and little financial capital. To use a golfing analogy, they are "short putts." Little is risked, and so the hurdle rate expected is low. On the other end of the spectrum are "game changers." These involve projects with a high degree of difference from the current business, which also require significant financial and human capital. They may require skills or IP not found in the current business, necessitating an acquisition or partnership. These are high risk and require a high expected rate of return as a result. The actual hurdle rate required in each box will vary by business.

Intelligent gambling leverages assets unique to large companies – financial capital and the ability to manage global complexity. Developing an Intelligent Gambler's mentality would give Dell a significant advantage in a competitive environment of extremely rapid change. First, partnering with smaller companies would allow Dell to avoid some of the "big-company" problems of bloat, bureaucracy, and internal focus identified by Collins. Second, technology is changing with increasing rapidity, as noted by Brynjolfsson and McAfee, and winners and losers are difficult to predict. Dell has significant cash at a time when venture capitalists are risk averse. Bets on technologies "close to home" (left side of the framework) will help create sustaining innovations that extend existing advantages, while bets in areas less related to the PC have potential to disrupt those industries. Dell can create competitive advantage by using its significant capital to make appropriate bets on diverse technologies. This is important because, in the digital era, winners and losers in a particular space are difficult to predict due to the pace of change. As Elaine Chin, chief wellness officer at Telus, told me, when asked to pick the future winners and losers in wearables, "It's like we're right at the beginning with mainframe computers – whomever we pick won't be around in five years. It won't be FitBit – the market dominant force in wearables today. They are coming up with incremental stuff – they don't have their eye on the guy down the street with the bioscan."

Dell's acquisitions since 2008 (the year after Michael returned as CEO) are plotted against the Intelligent Gambler© framework in Figures 7.2 and 7.3. Appendix B provides further details about each acquisition. Dell's acquisition activity in 2008 was fairly modest, consisting principally of a $1.4 billion purchase of EqualLogic, a maker of a type of storage called iSCSI. Dell's 2008 acquisitions are plotted on the Intelligent Gambler© framework in Figure 7.2.

Between 2008 and 2014, however, Dell acquired over 25 companies, as shown in Figure 7.3. Notably, Dell made 10 acquisitions in the infrastructure/cloud services space, including a $3.9 billion purchase of Perot Systems in 2009. In 2012, the company paid almost $2.4 billion for Quest Software, a maker of server and application performance management software. Finally, Dell made 3 additional security acquisitions during this period, including SonicWALL for $1 billion in 2012 and SecureWorks for $612 million in 2011. These acquisitions were a risk, due to their expense and the degree of difference from Dell's PC business – the beginning of a return to Dell's early value of risk-taking.

Most of Dell's acquisitions have been in the "game changers" box – high complexity, high degree of

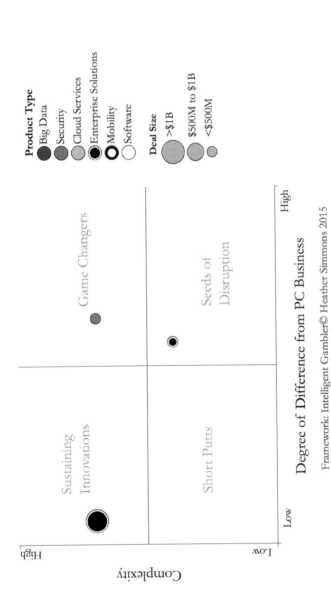

Figure 7.2. *Dell's acquisitions in 2008, as detailed in its annual reports and press releases, applied against the Intelligent Gambler© framework.*

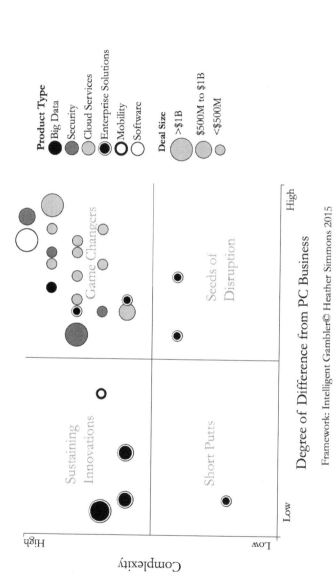

Figure 7.3. *Dell's acquisitions between 2008 and 2014, as detailed in its annual reports and press releases, applied against the Intelligent Gambler© framework.*

difference from the PC business. Importantly, Dell's massive customer base allows it to introduce these acquisitions to larger customer opportunities and to fuel their global expansion. Dell also has the power to combine innovations from this portfolio of acquisitions. For example, the threat data from SonicWALL's millions of appliance firewalls around the globe can be combined with the billions of cyber security events that SecureWorks sees every day to give Dell unprecedented insights into threats. By seeing more information on threats, Dell knows more and can then proactively protect its customers. By applying Brynjolffson and McAfee's "recombinant innovation" concept to its portfolio of acquisitions, Dell creates innovative solutions for customers and further leverages its advantages of scale, global complexity management, and significant cash flow. Dell has boldly refashioned its product strategy around these acquisitions, as will be discussed in a few pages.

My visit to Dell World in November 2014, along with a crowd of about 5,000 others, helped considerably in demonstrating just how far the company has shifted both its product focus and culture. At Dell World, Dell rolled out its new product strategy, designed to address the dizzying array of trends in the market today. In small group sessions, it also revealed its approach to regaining its risk-taker's culture.

Dell needs to regain its entrepreneurial spirit, while not losing all of the rigorous analytics and process that constitute the "guardrails" needed in a $60 billion company. It has begun to do so, although infusing this spirit throughout the organization will likely be an ongoing, challenging task, as cultures shift somewhat slowly. Some of the consultants have moved on, and Dell is bringing back more entrepreneurs in their place. Dell has recognized that innovation is vital to its future success and that it must re-develop a culture in which the benefits of risk-taking exceed the costs, from the employee's perspective. This was evident at Dell World, where Dell's classic openness and transparency was on full display. In response to a question I asked about his earlier comment that Dell employees had at one point been "afraid to fail," current Dell CFO Tom Sweet said, "We, for a number of years, fell into the trap of a management tone that said there wasn't enough reward for trying something and not quite getting there – it was more of a stick if you tried it and you didn't get there. And recognizing that that was beginning to stifle risk-taking, and you need some element of risk in a business – not everything's going to work. You just don't want it to be a disaster, by the way, so it has to be a thoughtful risk-reward thing. For a number of years, I think we fell into that trap, and then we lifted our heads up a few years ago and said, 'This isn't the way we're going to be successful.' Michael deserves a lot of credit for that ... You gotta have the culture and the tone at the top that says, 'We want this conversation. We're willing to change.'" In other words, Dell is re-creating an original shared value, namely risk-taking.

Sweet was part of a Dell World panel titled "Rethinking Innovation to Enhance the Customer Experience." It also included Rebekah Iliff, chief strategy officer of AirPR (a Dell partner); Jai Menon, Dell VP and chief research officer; Mike Cote, VP and general manager, Dell SecureWorks; and Jim Luisser, managing director of Dell Ventures. Kicking off the panel, Rebekah said, "[It] really has to do with entrepreneurship, and acquiring the skills and expertise to continue to innovate at this rapid pace. Within the organization now, it's no longer a question of 'Do we need to innovate'? It's 'How do we make innovation central to the organization, and how do we move faster?'"

Some of the innovation is coming from new acquisitions, such as SecureWorks. Cote said, "Innovation is going to come from multiple sources: the guys who are paid to sit around and think about 'n+2' [i.e., beyond next generation] technology, and also from your front-line people, the people who are doing things, who see how we could do things differently and better. Figuring out how to get that feedback into the organization and up [is key]. And, as we've all said, the 'failure' word is not a bad word." Indeed, "failure" allows companies to learn from mistakes and pivot as needed in new directions.

Cote's organization, now called Dell SecureWorks, was purchased by Dell in 2011. The company was not integrated into Dell, and headquarters remained in Atlanta. As one current employee said to me after I commented on the stepped-up pace of Dell's acquisitions, "Yes, and we no longer just absorb them like the Borg," the fictional alien race in *Star Trek* that assimilated other races. Dell is not just purchasing start-ups' ability to innovate, but also their willingness to innovate, leaving their agility and entrepreneurial spirit intact.

Guardrails for managing risk remain in place, although the shift back to an entrepreneurial culture was much in evidence at Dell World. For example, new "innovation councils" fund pilot projects and review execution against defined milestones every month. Tom Sweet also commented about Cote's organization, "After Michael said 'Grow, and we'll give you as much capital as you need,' the one thing I added to that was, 'And by the way, you have to generate one dollar of cash flow in that growth strategy.' That was my quid pro quo in that conversation." In other words, Dell is re-creating a shared value, rapid execution, while maintaining some guardrails or rules of engagement.

The return to hiring entrepreneurs, and the stepped-up pace of acquisitions, may increase creative abrasion, creative resolution, and creative agility at Dell. In short, it could increase Dell's ability to innovate. This ability to innovate is reflected in Dell's substantially revamped product line. At Dell World, I was quite surprised to see the degree to which Dell has shifted its product direction beyond commodity PCs and related services and towards higher-margin, higher-growth businesses that have not commoditized. While execution on this strategic shift remains, the strategy, at least, is in place.

As highlighted at Dell World, Dell's four technology focus areas are cloud, big data, mobile, and security. In their breakout sessions and technology showcases, Dell also highlighted partnerships associated with the Internet of Things (i.e., connectivity and intelligence in everyday items such as cars and refrigerators), and it is now selling 3D printers made by MakerBot. Dell restated its commitment to end-to-end computing (providing everything that an information technology customer needs – from PCs to servers to cloud to software to service). Dell is most definitely not getting out of the PC business, which still provides the entry point for 70% of its new customers.[1]

Figure 7.4. *Dell's product showcase, featuring big data and the Internet of Things ("IOT").*

Dell's newer markets, however, each represent profit pools approaching the size of, or larger than, PCs. The Agile Product Portfolio framework, shown in Figure 7.5, illuminates the need for large corporations to continually invest in these newer opportunities with high growth potential and to couple those with some sort of cash cow or Trojan Horse business that both pays the bills and allows access to a larger customer set.

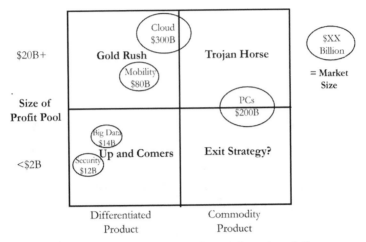

Figure 7.5. Author's Agile Product Portfolio
framework depicting Dell's revamped product
mix. Support for each calculation in Figure 7.5 is
in Appendix A.

At a high level, Dell's product strategy is
differentiated from that of HP and IBM in that, first,
Dell is the only major IT player providing end-to-end
computing. End-to-end computing is the provision of
complete IT solutions, from PCs to servers, software,
data management, security, and the cloud. IBM sold
its PC business to Lenovo years ago, and in October
2014, HP announced a decision to spin off its PC
business. Dell is therefore leveraging assets it uniquely
has, such as a complete mix of software, services,
PCs, enterprise products, and direct relationships
with many enterprise customers. Once Dell is in
these enterprise accounts, it can sell customers its

newer higher-margin products, such as security. Dell is also leveraging its massive advantages of scale ($50 billion+ in revenues) and ability to manage complexity (111,000 employees).

Dell is often already a recognized industry leader (in capability if not in market share) in these product categories, frequently due to a savvy acquisition. For example, in managed security services, Dell SecureWorks is positioned in Gartner's Leaders Quadrant, ahead of IBM, HP, Cisco, and Juniper.[2] Gartner noted Dell's Counter Threat unit's security expertise, and its relationship management, as strengths. Gartner also positions Dell in the Leaders Quadrant for private cloud and for Platform-As-A-Service.[3] Gartner highlights Dell Boomi, a software platform that facilitates simple "point and click" integration of other applications in the cloud. A detailed analysis of Dell's new target markets and products is in Appendix A, with indications of Dell's position relative to competitors (according to Gartner, IDC, etc.).

Within these product categories, Dell focuses on open standards rather than proprietary solutions. For example, in the cloud arena, Dell is co-developing offerings that run on Red Hat's Linux OpenStack platform, instead of developing their own public cloud, as HP and IBM did.[4] Dell's Cloud Marketplace, for example, is an easy-to-use, vendor-agnostic platform that allows customers to choose the best cloud solution for their needs.

Dell's new product strategy leverages its strengths (scale, capital, and an existing beachhead in business accounts – namely, PCs), while making bets in differentiated, higher-margin product categories. These bets will allow Dell to continue to innovate, rather than simply cut costs to become the low-cost player in a pure commodity market (PCs). It also allows plenty of upside for growth. Dell's market share in each of the security, big data, and mobility (tablet) markets is less than 5%,[5,6,7] and it has just under 12% share[8] in the cloud infrastructure market, compared to about 13%[9] share in PCs.

With this new product strategy, Dell is demonstrating creative resolution. This strategy has elements of both product/service innovation and business model innovation. For example, Dell SecureWorks launches Dell out of the commodity hardware business and into the higher-margin, faster-growth security software business, complete with counter-threat intelligence experts and security operations centers around the globe. When Dell acquired SecureWorks in 2011, SecureWorks was processing 13 billion cyber events per day. By early 2014, that number had grown to 70 billion cyber events per day,[10] and at that growth rate is likely about 120 billion daily cyber events today. Security software is clearly a significant product innovation.

Dell's cloud focus, however, has elements of business model innovation. For example, in November 2014, it announced Cloud Marketplace, a portal that allows developers and IT managers to "compare, purchase, use, and manage" public cloud services and applications from Amazon, Google, Salesforce, Taleo, and others. The portal is vendor-agnostic and self-service. Recognizing that it is unlikely to be able to compete with Amazon, Google, and the like in providing public cloud services, Dell has become a vendor-agnostic distributor of those services. It is in essence renting hardware to end users, and selling hardware to cloud providers. By building strong partnerships with Amazon, Google, Salesforce, and others, Dell ensures that its servers, storage, and PCs serve as the backend infrastructure in those clouds. Dell has chosen to innovate in both IT-related products and services, and in the business model that allows it to distribute those products and services where it does not have an advantage in the product/ service itself. The significant shift in Dell's product and services mix is shown in Figure 7.6.

One of my thesis advisors, reading the first draft of the thesis upon which this book is based, said

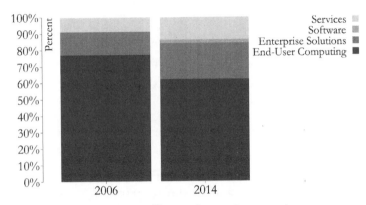

*Figure 7.6. Dell's product mix over time,
according to its annual reports.*

that I "sounded like a 14-year-old schoolboy with a
crush on Madonna" in my enthusiasm for Dell's new
product strategy (my advisors are a staid bunch).
He insisted that I find the weakness in it. Well, that's
easy. As noted in Chapter 6, Dell clearly was late
in transitioning to mobile devices such as tablets,
although it now has a tablet, the Dell Venue. It is not
in the top five in tablet market share. Tablets are a
hardware product that will likely commoditize like
PCs did (making relatively early market entry the
only hope of making significant profits). However,
Dell chooses to be in the tablet business since tablets
are complementary products to notebooks, in that
users can now perform many computing tasks on a
tablet, such as surfing the internet or sending email.
Dell appears to be focusing its mobility offerings on

consulting and offering security products associated with the increasing "bring your own device" ("BYOD") trend in corporations, in which employees bring their own mobile phones and tablets to work rather than being issued a corporate version. Dell's lack of strength in mobility is a weakness in its vastly improved product portfolio.

As I wrote the final draft of my thesis in early 2015, this news arrived: Dell wins the 2015 Consumer Electronics Show ("CES") "Best of Innovation" award and "Best Mobile Device" award for the Dell Venue tablet. The world's thinnest tablet comes with an "edge-to-edge" Infinity Display and a camera that allows you to manipulate pictures and apply real-time filters to them. Sigh. Never bet against Michael Dell. It's just a bad idea.

The discussion of tablets as complementary products for PCs brings us to the topic of wearables, which are complementary products for tablets (for example, the Jawbone Up24 fitness band output is read on a tablet or smartphone). Miniaturization is now allowing computers to be worn. Dell is investigating new computing form factors (one of the breakout sessions I attended featured a Dell partner who was developing a wearable health monitoring device for seniors), but at Dell World I did not see as much emphasis on wearables as the market opportunity might dictate. This stands as an opportunity yet to be addressed as Dell remakes itself. The wearables market is growing at over 60% year on year and will be a $19 billion market within the next few years.[11] The market is fragmented, as the PC market was 25 years ago, creating an opportunity for larger players to consolidate and enhance it. An Intelligent Gambler might apply Dell's new expertise in security to address privacy concerns associated with wearables, for example. While there are already companies developing wearable fitness and entertainment devices for the consumer, there have been fewer applications developed for the business and government markets, Dell's strength. Margins exceed 50%, compared to sub-10% for PCs.[12]

So Dell has substantially revamped its product line as part of its strategy to reinvent itself. How is it addressing its damaged reputation for customer service? First, Dell continues to focus on enterprise customers (business and government) over the consumer. Dell has wisely chosen not to storm Apple's consumer citadel, much as it chooses not to compete head on with Amazon and Google in public cloud services. Most of the discussion about the consumer at Dell focuses on the "consumerization of IT,"[13] which means the trend of consumers bringing their

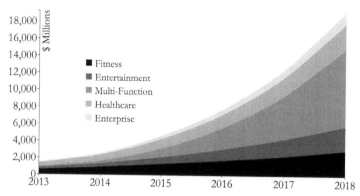

Figure 7.7. Wearables hardware and services revenue forecast.[11]

own devices to work. Consumers remain about 20% of Dell's customer mix, and Dell continues to view that as an "opportunistic" market (meaning, Dell will sell to consumers, but it is not the company's focus). As Michael Dell said in a September 2014 interview with CNBC:

> We're bringing powerful solutions to our customers which are generally businesses and institutions. We have a consumer business but there's been a lot of focus at Dell on building solutions across the whole spectrum. So this is a combination of hardware, software, services together, to be able to virtualize an environment, build out a cloud data center, enable a salesforce to be productive but secure at the same time.[14]

This shapes Dell's services offerings primarily towards the needs of enterprise customers, who typically require less hand-holding.

Second, in terms of creating a competitive advantage in service, I think that Dell will leverage big data internally to create a better customer experience. Because Dell sold directly to the end customer, Dell always had better data on what that customer bought and how often, and what their service history was. In one of the Dell World breakout sessions I attended, Dell managers talked about using their data advantage to create "smart" products that will tell the customer when they need maintenance or are about to fail. This idea has come to fruition as Dell ProSupport launched in early 2015 (I better get this book out). For an IT manager, replacing a hard drive that is about to fail is a thirty-minute inconvenience. Replacing one after it has failed (with a user who has probably not backed up all his data) is far more disruptive. Moving forward, I think that Dell can provide easy-to-use, low-cost, and smart (predictive) products to strengthen their end-to-end relationship with customers. It can also leverage social media, such as Twitter, to rapidly and cost-effectively deal with service issues, taking back the conversation from the Dell Hell forums that exploded in the mid-2000s. While turning around its service reputation will take time, predictive maintenance and use of social media provide a solid start.

Dell has also shifted its business model strategy to include more sales through the channel. Dell, which originally built its business on cutting out the middleman, now sells 40% of its products through intermediaries. This "omnichannel" approach more closely matches the needs and buying preferences of its customers, who prefer to go through a partner procurement process 70% of the time.[15]

Dell has thus revamped its product, service, and business model strategy, reaffirming its commitment to the PC and end-to-end computing. Its new value proposition has elements of the old – low-cost products and services – and the new – "smart" services like predictive maintenance, some critical expertise and IP in security, and channel sales.

The final strategic shift deals with the pressures of Wall Street. The debate about whether Dell should remain a public company or go private was played out visibly in the press in a battle between Michael Dell and Carl Icahn. Ultimately, Michael Dell won shareholder support and took the company private in the fall of 2013. CFO Sweet said about going private, "I think it was a very symbolic step. Michael loves to talk about the fact that he's no longer on a ninety-day cycle. The fact of the matter is, I'm still on a ninety-day cycle, because I'm still talking to all the debt people, the analysts, but he's not. But I do think it was a catalyst, to leapfrog that conversation forward, as a demonstration to the organization."

Innovation is likely to increase now that Dell is a private company. A July 2014 study by Shai Bernstein at the Stanford Graduate School of Business concluded that going public caused a decline in the novelty of patent filings (as measured by the number of citations a patent receives after it is approved) but not the number of patent filings, suggesting that transitioning to the public equity markets causes firms to reposition their R&D portfolio towards more conventional projects.[16] A similar working paper at INSEAD (working title "Entrepreneurial Exits and Innovation") also found that innovation quality was highest under private ownership and lowest under public ownership, again using patents as the measure.[17] Hsu and Aggarwal found that the reason for this was "information disclosure" – since public companies are required to report their results, managers back safer, more core projects in order to produce results in the short term.[18] Risk-taking becomes easier when failures are not broadcast. Aggarwal discusses Dell's "going private" transaction:

> Dell is a great example: One of the reasons they've been less innovative over the past decade or so is because they've been under constant public scrutiny. Part of the motivation behind the

buyout is to spur innovation at all levels of the company.[18]

The 2012 study "Incentives to Innovate and the Decision to Go Public or Private," by Daniel Ferreira, Gustavo Manso, and Andre Silva, also concludes that private firms are more innovative:

> Private firms take more risks, invest in new products and technologies, and pursue more radical innovations. Private firms are more likely to choose projects that are complex, difficult to describe, and untested ... Mergers and acquisitions, divestitures, and changes in organizational structure and management practices are more easily motivated under private ownership.[19]

Finally, going private reduces the obsession with growth that is built into the stock prices of fast-growth companies such as Dell. This obsession with growth, as pointed out by author Jim Collins, leads to short-term thinking as companies try to hit growth targets, and an internal focus as companies constantly reorganize in an attempt to seek incremental growth at the lowest cost.

The remaining question is whether Dell should stay private or return to the public markets. My own analysis bears out the benefits of Dell staying private. Using the information in Dell's filings with the Securities and Exchange Commission ("SEC") at

the time it went private, it is possible to estimate the
relative revenue and profit contribution of its core PC
business (desktops and notebooks), its core Enterprise
Solutions business (servers, storage, and services),
and its newer businesses (cloud, tablets, security,
enterprise software, etc.). For the information of my
fellow accountants, I am using operating income as
the profit measure – everyone else, just think plain
old "profits," or revenues minus costs. The SEC filings
and the work of consultants Boston Consulting
Group ("BCG") and J.P. Morgan also allowed me
to estimate growth rates for each product category,
under both "stay private" and "go public again"
scenarios.[20] Product categories in Figures 7.8 and 7.9
include "Commodity Core" (desktops, notebooks,
peripherals, and related services), "Enterprise
Core" (servers, storage, and related services), and
"Innovation" (infrastructure, cloud and security
services, applications and business process services,
software, and tablets). Details for supporting
assumptions and sources for the scenarios are in
Appendix C. Figure 7.8 depicts the revenue scenarios.

Dell's estimated 2013 revenues (it went private
in fall of 2013) were $57 billion[23] with estimated
operating income of about $2.3 billion.[24, 25] If Dell
goes public within a year or two, by 2023, it could be
a $56 billion company (revenues) with about

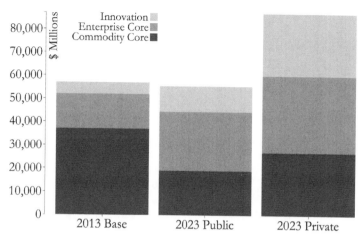

Figure 7.8. *Dell's projected 2023 revenues under "go public" and "stay private" scenarios. Source: Author's analysis and various research reports.*[20, 21,22]

$3.6 billion in profits. This assumes a compound annual growth rate shrinkage of about .3% per year, driven by a 6% annual shrinkage in its core PC business,[26] which is not completely offset by significant growth in more innovative businesses. On the other hand, if Dell stays private and invests in the growth of innovation-driven businesses such as security, big data, cloud, and mobility, by 2023, it could be an $87 billion business (4-5% CAGR), with $6 billion in profits. (Of course, I could be wrong. Michael's always liked nice round numbers.) Figure 7.9 depicts the profit scenarios.

Most of the revenue and profit growth in the "stay private" scenarios is accounted for by an estimated

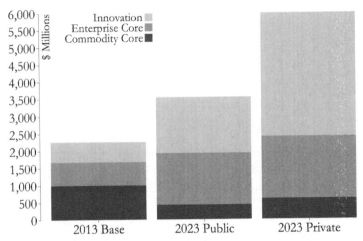

Figure 7.9. *Dell's projected 2023 profits under "go public" and "stay private" scenarios. Source: Author's analysis, various research reports.*[20, 21, 22]

18% revenue CAGR in Dell's innovation-driven product lines. This rate is 1.5X the growth rate[27] of those innovation-driven markets, namely security, big data, mobility, and cloud. As examples of growth rates in these markets, the security services market growth is projected to be 15.4% between 2013 and 2019,[28] and the business intelligence (big data) market grew 8% in 2013.[29] Further details of growth rates by market are in Appendix A. For those doubting that a very large company can grow total revenues in the 4-5% range, Dell grew at a CAGR of 11.6% during the period 2004-2006, when it was a $50 billion company. Apple had $183 billion in revenues in 2014, and grew at about 7%.[30] The important conclusion in this sea of numbers? I argue that Dell's 2023 profit could be 70% higher if it stays private rather than goes public again.

Dell is now the third-largest private company in the world, behind Cargill and Koch Industries.[31] And based on Michael Dell's comments about the benefits of not being on a ninety-day clock, Dell seems unlikely to go public again anytime soon. Will it go public, and if so, when? Let's start with why companies in general go public. Companies go public because they need capital, an enhanced reputation with customers, or a boost to their brand. Dell had about $12 billion in cash[32] when it went private and strong cash flow. Dell does not need capital, and it has a leading share amongst its enterprise customer base as well as a well-recognized brand. Also, the stock market did not recognize Dell's shift in product mix or record revenue performance in its fiscal year 2012, before Dell went private. The stock actually declined in 2012. The conclusion? Dell has no reason to go public again.

Will Dell eventually be forced to go public to create liquidity for the principal investors? Michael Dell provided $4.2 billion or 75% of the equity in the buyout, and Silver Lake contributed $1.4 billion or 25% of the equity.[33] The remainder of the

$24.9 billion buyout price consisted of $18 billion in debt and some of Dell's cash.[34] Dell paid down its debt by $3.4 billion last year, using its strong cash flow. This resulted in Standard & Poor's (debt rating agency) upgrading Dell's corporate credit rating by two notches and upgrading its senior unsecured debt by three notches.[35] The price of Dell's debt has risen by about 60% since it went private, through the spring of 2015.

Debt investors, therefore, are getting repaid. On the equity side, if Michael Dell or Silver Lake requires liquidity, the company can issue dividends from its cash flow, so there is no need for Dell to go public in order to provide ongoing liquidity for these investors. However, Silver Lake may eventually want to exit its Dell holdings entirely, in order to provide a realized gain for investors in its fund. Indeed, the estimated value of Michael Dell and Silver Lake's equity holdings rose from $5.6 billion in 2013, at the buyout, to $10.8 billion less than a year later.[36] That is over a 90% gain on the equity alone, in one year. It is an impressive gain, but it is only a gain on paper until someone buys Silver Lake out. Typical holding periods for private equity funds are at least five years,[37] which puts a likely Silver Lake exit sometime after 2018. There is, however, no need to go public in order to buy Silver Lake out. Given the relative proportion of their equity holdings and Michael Dell's other assets, Michael could buy Silver Lake out himself, or the company could do it, again from cash flow. It's also unlikely that Dell will be sold privately to another firm. Given the size of the $24.9 billion buyout in 2013 and the possible 70% increase in profits by 2023, the price would likely be a steep $40 billion. Nine of the ten largest high-tech acquisitions of all time were for less than $20 billion.[38] Given that Dell has no need to tap the public markets and is unlikely to be purchased by another firm, it will likely remain a private company, with Michael Dell as the principal shareholder.

Whew. I'm calling it now, in August 2015. Dell stays private. By the early 2020s, revenues are $90 billion or so. Profits are $6 to $7 billion. Dell is recognized as one of the world's most innovative firms. Go ahead and call me crazy. You'll be buying the beers.

"Dell's promising third act is built on the bitter lessons of its second."

—Heather Simmons

EIGHT

A Few Suggestions

IN SUMMARY, DELL HAS DONE much to reinvent itself and shift its product, service, and business model strategy. It has expanded its product portfolio to include security, cloud, big data, and mobility offerings. Many of those new product offerings were brought into the fold as Dell "intelligently gambled" by purchasing over 25 companies. At the same time, Dell has reaffirmed its commitment to providing its customers with "end-to-end" computing – including PCs. It is using data and predictive analytics to provide more proactive and "smart" support to enterprise customers, and embracing an "omnichannel" approach to provide those customers with flexibility in how they buy their products and services. It has escaped the crushing pressures and short-term thinking of Wall Street by going private.

Impressively, and perhaps most importantly, Dell has also put in place many elements required to recreate its original entrepreneurial, risk-taker's culture – an organization both willing and able to innovate. The cultural change is arguably the most crucial, as it will allow Dell to continue to innovate as required over time. It is indeed "the soft stuff" that will make or break Dell's reinvention, projected on Hill, et al.'s, framework in Figure 8.1.

Will these changes be enough for Dell to return to phenomenal performance in an age of exponential acceleration of innovation? What else is needed? I was rarely the smartest guy in the room at Dell (and when I was, I was usually alone). However, here are a few of my additional recommendations for Dell.

First, Dell should fly its freak flag in hiring, at all levels. Urban Dictionary defines the term "fly your freak flag" as: "A characteristic, mannerism, or appearance of a person, either subtle or overt, which implies unique, eccentric, creative, adventurous or unconventional thinking."[1] As noted in Chapter 4, intellectual diversity has been critical in some of the biggest innovations of our time. And as identified in Chapter 6, Dell's massive influx of people, including many consultants, helped result in a culture that tilted too far away from entrepreneurial execution and towards process-oriented analysis. Hire some creative people, some statisticians, and some artists and designers, and mix them into the business units.

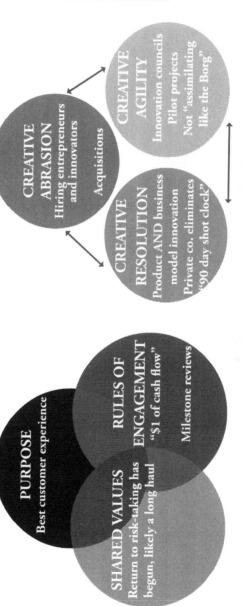

Figure 8.1. Dell's current position on Hill, et al.'s "Willing and Able to Innovate" framework, as depicted by the author.

Second, Dell should hire managers who listen and who encourage risk-taking and thoughtful failure. Train them to be Intelligent Gamblers and establish regular reviews and incentives to ensure some of these new technology ideas get funded. As author Robert Sutton says, reward failure and success but punish inaction.[2] This will be the hardest part of the transition to the "world's largest start-up," because employees have long memories and related stories (which are told and retold) of the days when risk-taking was not encouraged.

Third, stay private. Staying private produces superior revenues and profits, relative to going public again.

Fourth, combine big data and the cloud to further simplify IT and improve Dell's service reputation. Dell could, for example, extend its predictive analytics advantage in services by making its products predictive and *self-healing,* combining the power of the cloud, software-as-a-service models, and big data. Not only could the hard drive notify you that it was about to fail, but the system could diagnose the problem in real-time and run the appropriate "correcting" software (like anti-virus, or defragmenter) immediately, without user intervention. It could also automatically back up your system for you, to the cloud. The faulty system could notify Dell that there is an issue and order the appropriate replacement part. Adding self-healing capabilities moves services powered by predictive analytics from the "sustaining innovations" box to the "game changers" box on the Intelligent Gambler© framework, because it requires some investment in companies that are dissimilar to the existing PC business.

Fifth, invest human and financial capital into simplifying IT for small and medium businesses ("SMB"), which must make choices about the dizzying array of options for phones, faxes, computers, cloud services, security, and application software. Dell could, for example, extend its Cloud Marketplace idea to create an SMB Marketplace, which provides SMBs with guidance as to the right phone, fax, PC, cloud, security, and application providers for their needs. SMBs can select the products and services needed, bundle them with PCs or tablets, and order the entire bundle directly from the SMB Marketplace. Cash-crunched SMBs could even select an option to pay a single monthly "per seat" charge for these bundles, with no long-term contracts, using Dell Financial Services as the financing arm. At the end of a certain period of use, say three years, Dell could automatically pick up any old PC hardware and install upgraded versions, simplifying life for the SMB and creating annuity revenues and long-term relationships for Dell. Long-term relationships in this sector are highly profitable for Dell – Dell's SMB segment had 11.2% operating income for the fiscal year ended February 1, 2013, compared to 8.7% for Dell's large enterprise segment, 8.3% for the public (government) segment, and negative operating income for the consumer segment.[3] Adding an array of new products, services, and financing options for small business moves the Cloud Marketplace concept from the "seeds of disruption" box to the "game changers" box on the Intelligent Gambler© framework, because of the additional complexity and capital required to integrate multiple products into a single bundled offering.

Sixth, find a way to invest in enterprise wearables, or at least experiment with them in a small way. Wearables may cannibalize smartphones and tablets, like those technologies cannibalized the PC industry. Best to be ahead of, rather than behind, that trend. Go ahead and start that "parking lot conversation" – and then follow through.

In sum, Dell's promising third act is built on the bitter lessons of its second. Dell has put in place many of the elements required to resolve the conflicts of its challenging middle period, and to re-establish the organization's willingness and ability to innovate, in an era in which innovation is more crucial than ever before. Now all it has to do is execute. And if you don't know whether Dell can do that, you may not have been following along.

Postscript

IN OCTOBER 2015, as this book was going to print, *The Wall Street Journal* ("WSJ") announced that Dell was in merger talks with EMC, a leading provider of storage, cloud, software, and data solutions. EMC has a market valuation of over $50 billion. A day later, the WSJ announced that Dell had quietly filed for an IPO of its security business, SecureWorks. The WSJ said that Dell believed it could generate $2 billion from this IPO, on a $612 million investment just four years earlier. Sources said that the cash could be used to fund additional acquisitions. Suffice to say that these two moves would be game changers for Dell.

This book launched three weeks later. As my dad always told me, "Sometimes, Heather, it's better to be lucky than smart." Thanks, Dad, and I'm sure you meant it as a compliment.

Acknowledgments

THIS BOOK WOULD NOT HAVE come alive without the help of my friends and former colleagues at Dell. First, I am grateful to three lifelong friends who worked with me at Dell. They pored through their archives and dug up reams of old press clippings and photos for this effort. More importantly, without them, I would not have been able to accomplish half of what I did at Dell. While they remain unnamed, you know these people if you've ever worked at Dell and heard, "Really? I'm sure she didn't mean that. Her bark is much worse than her bite." Thanks for the air cover, guys.

My former colleagues, including Tom Martin, Indraj Gill, Bill Sharpe, and several others who chose to remain anonymous, generously shared their Dell memories and considerable powers of analysis with me. My interviews with them, as well as with Telus executive Elaine Chin, form the heart of this book. They were, in Dell terms, part of the group of "pioneers" who built the company. They were all simply vital in helping Dell become the company it was. In addition, my conversation with Tom Martin sparked the idea that became the Intelligent Gambler© framework. He's always been the smartest guy in the room.

I can't forget my OCADU thesis supervisors, the irrepressible Suzanne Stein and Eric Blais. Not only are they both blessed with big brains, they are also diligent, thorough, and wickedly funny. They see things and make connections that others do not. They made my thesis, and hence this book, markedly better.

Speaking of OCADU, my former classmates Katie Meyer and Dushan Milic graced this book with their editing and design skills, respectively. Such talent. Nerds rule.

My former HBS professor Dr. Linda Hill and her co-authors penned *Collective Genius* and gave the world the "Willing and Able to Innovate" framework for assessing an organization's readiness to innovate. It is a very practical and complete framework, and it is used in this book to analyze shifts in Dell's culture and capacity for innovation.

Finally, to the Dell executive who took the time to review a few pages of this book: thanks for pointing out the power of combining acquisitions in the Intelligent Gambler© framework, for walking me through the logic of why companies go public, and for making sure I did not leave out the cash conversion cycle. Thanks to you, this book's a little smarter than I am.

Appendices

APPENDIX A: DETAILED NEW MARKETS ANALYSIS

Note: Appendix A assesses the new product markets Dell has recently entered. It follows HBS professor Michael Porter's "Five Forces" framework for analyzing markets and competitive strategies.[1]

	Security Outsourcing	Big Data	Cloud	Mobility (Tablets)	PCs
Market Size	$12 billion ("B")[2]	$14.4B[5]	$155B for public cloud[8] $32B for private cloud[9] $143B for data centre[10]	250 million tablet units or $70-80B[13]	315 million units[16] or roughly $200B[17]
Growth	15.4% through 2017[2]	8% in 2013[5]	20% for public cloud[9] 40-50% for private cloud[9]	11-12% for 2014[13]	-.2% for 2014[16]
Operating Margin	18-50%[3]	Roughly 30%[6]	Approximately 20-25%[11]	About 25%[14]	<5%[17]
Profit Pools	$3B (calculated as $12B X 25% operating margin)	$4.5B (calculated)	$50B+ (calculated)	$18B (calculated)	$10B (calculated)
Buyer Power	High for large corporations, moderate for small/mid sized businesses ("SMBs")	High, typically large corporations	High, cost conscious	High	High
Threat of Substitution	Moderate – cloud-based offerings	Low – learning curve	Low to moderate, in-house IT	High – smartphones, phablets	High – tablets, smartphones

	Security Outsourcing	Big Data	Cloud	Mobility (Tablets)	PCs
Supplier Power	Low – only suppliers are for servers, storage, energy, and other commodities	Low	Moderate, electrical power may become constrained	Low	Low – commodity products
Competitors	Verizon, IBM, HP, Symantec (large business) Checkpoint, Fortinet, Sophos, Cisco, Juniper (SMB)	IBM, SAS, Oracle, Tableau, Microsoft	Amazon, Google, Rackspace, AT&T in public cloud. IBM, HP, others in private cloud	Apple, Samsung, Asus, Lenovo, Amazon	Lenovo, HP, Acer, Apple
Dell Position	Gartner Leaders quadrant for both SMB and large business, ahead of IBM, HP, Cisco, Juniper[4]	Not in Gartner Leaders Quadrant[7]	Gartner Leaders Quadrant for data center outsourcing (private cloud) along with HP and IBM.[12] Does not compete in public cloud with Amazon, Google, etc.	Not in top 5 in market share[15]	#3 worldwide with 13% market share[16]

	Security Outsourcing	Big Data	Cloud	Mobility (Tablets)	PCs
Barriers to New Entry	High – big data analytics and expertise required	High – insights required	High – requires scale	High – requires scale	High – consoli-dated, requires scale

APPENDIX B: LIST OF DELL'S ACQUISITIONS

Note: Appendix B provides details on Dell's acquisitions between 2008 and 2014.

Appendix B

Acquisition	Description	Type	Year	Price
EqualLogic	iSCSI storage	Enterprise Solutions Group ("ESG")	2008	$1.4 billion ("B")
Message One	SaaS for compliance, archiving, and disaster recovery	Security	2008	$164 million ("M")
The Networked Storage Company	Transitioning storage network infrastructure	ESG	2008	Undisclosed
Perot Systems	IT consulting services	Cloud	2009	$3.9B
Allin Microsoft Services	Designing scalable networks and application architectures	ESG	2009	$12M
Kace	Management ("mgt") appliances device discovery, SW distribution, patch mgt	Mobility	2010	Undisclosed
Scalent	Datacenter infrastructure/workload mgt	Cloud	2010	Undisclosed
Boomi	Cloud application management software – allows easy transfer of data between cloud-based and on-premise applications.	Cloud	2010	Undisclosed
InSite One	Cloud-based medical archiving software and storage of medical images, with disaster recovery	Cloud	2010	Undisclosed

APPENDIX B CONTINUED

Acquisition	Description	Type	Year	Price
Ocarina Networks	Storage compression and content-aware de-duplication. Data management	ESG	2010	Undisclosed
Exanet	Clustered network-attached storage ("NAS")	ESG	2010	$12M
Compellent	Mid-range fibre channel storage	ESG	2011	$960M
Force10	Data center networking – switches and routers	ESG	2011	$700M
SecureWorks	SaaS managed security services	Security	2011	$612M
RNA Networks	Server and memory virtualization technology	ESG	2011	Undisclosed
Quest Software	Server, access, and application performance management	Software	2012	$2.4B
SonicWALL	Security appliances and management, back-up and recovery	Security	2012	$1B
Make Technologies	Application modernization software and services. Application re-engineering. Runs most effectively on open, standardized platforms including the cloud	Cloud	2012	Undisclosed

Appendix B

Acquisition	Description	Type	Year	Price
Credant Technologies	Data protection from endpoints, to service, storage, and the cloud	Security	2012	Undisclosed
AppAssure	Server, data, and application backup and recovery for virtual, physical, and cloud infrastructures	Security	2012	Undisclosed
Gale Technologies	Deployment and infrastructure mgt for on-premise and hybrid clouds	Cloud	2012	Undisclosed
Clerity Solutions	Application modern-ization and re-hosting; Transitions business critical applications and data from legacy systems to modern architectures, including the cloud	Cloud	2012	Undisclosed
Wyse Technology	Thin client solutions with advanced management, desktop virtualization, and cloud software.	Cloud	2012	Undisclosed
Enstratius	Cloud-infrastructure management for public, private and hybrid-cloud deployments, either SaaS or on-premise	Cloud	2013	Undisclosed
Statsoft	Predictive analytics	Big Data	2014	Undisclosed

Source: Dell annual reports and website, news reports.[1]

APPENDIX C: PUBLIC VS. PRIVATE SCENARIOS SUPPORTING DETAIL

Note: Appendix C provides supporting detail for the future revenue and profit projections for Dell under both public company and private company scenarios.

Appendix C

Revenues ($M): Public Company	2013	2023	CAGR	Notes and Sources
Innovation Group	$5,000	$11,000	8.2%	• Dell infrastructure, cloud, security services revenues were $2.4 billion ("B") annualized in 2013.[1] • Dell applications and business process services revenues were $1.2B annualized in 2013.[1] • Dell software revenues were $1.2B annualized in 2013.[1] • Dell tablet revenues were roughly $500 million ("M") in 2013.[2] • Total Innovation Group revenues estimated at $5B for 2013 (roughly sum of above). • CAGR estimated at about 8% based on Dell infrastructure/ cloud services 2013 growth rate of 8%, consistent with low end of market rate of 8-17%.[3,4,5]
Enterprise Core	$15,000	$25,500	5.4%	• Dell Enterprise Services Group ("ESG") annualized 2013 revenues $13B, with annualized ESG portion of services revenues $1.2B.[1] • Total Dell Enterprise Core revenue therefore estimated at $15B for 2013. • CAGR estimated at about 5%. Boston Consulting Group ("BCG") estimated Dell's ESG revenue growth at 5.1% in base case scenario for Dell Board.[6]

Revenues ($M): Public Company	2013	2023	CAGR	Notes and Sources
Commodity Core	$37,000	$19,000	-6.4%	• Dell End User Computing ("EUC") annualized revenues of $35B for 2013, net of tablet revenue. Annualized EUC portion of services revenues $3.5B.[1] • Total 2013 EUC revenues estimated at $37B, consistent with BCG estimates. • BCG assumes EUC shrinks at 6% CAGR.[6]
Total Public Revenues	$57,000	$55,500	-.3%	• 2013 Dell revenues estimated at approximately $57B.[7]

Revenues ($M): Private Company	2013	2023	CAGR	Notes and Sources
Innovation Group	$5,000	$27,000	18.4%	• Michael Dell has said he would like to double the size of the combined businesses represented by Innovation Group and Enterprise Core, by 2019.[8] That growth rate implies these businesses will be about $60B combined by 2023. • 18% CAGR assumed as a private company, or about 1.5X market growth.[3,4,5]
Enterprise Core	$15,000	$33,000	8.2%	• Dell server revenue grew 5.7% in 2014,[9] and storage revenue grew 14.3% in the first half of 2014.[10] Servers are about 85% of ESG revenue.[1] • Dell Enterprise Core CAGR therefore estimated at roughly 8%.
Commodity Core	$37,000	$27,000	-3.1%	• Dell grew PC units 10.3% in 2014.[11] PC average selling prices ("ASPs") decline about 10% per year.[12] • 3% annual decline assumed in Commodity revenues due to assumed pricing aggressiveness as a private company (i.e., ASPs decline more than 10%).
Total Private Revenues	$57,000	$87,000	4.3%	

APPENDIX C CONTINUED

Operating Income ("Op Inc") ($M): Public Co.	2013	2023	2013 Op Inc %	2023 Op Inc %	Notes and Sources
Innovation Group	$585	$1,625	11.7%	14.8%	• Combined operating income ("op inc") for Dell Software and Services was 11.6% in first half of 2013. Services alone was 16.7%, with Software negative.[13] 11.7% assumed. • Software should reverse its negative margins. Op inc therefore assumed to grow 2-3 points faster than revenue for this group under public scenario. Assumed op inc CAGR of 10.8% results in 2023 op inc of $1.625B, or a 14.8% op inc percentage.
Enterprise Core	$675	$1,500	4.5%	5.9%	• Op inc of 4.3% in ESG as of Aug 2, 2013,[14] grows at 5-8% per year.[15] • Assumed 8.3% op inc CAGR yields 2023 op inc of $1.5B, or 5.9% of sales.

Operating Income ("Op Inc") ($M): Public Co.	2013	2023	2013 Op Inc %	2023 Op Inc %	Notes and Sources
Commodity Core	$1,000	$425	2.7%	2.2%	• Op inc of 2.4% in EUC as of August 2, 2013.[16] 2.7% assumed. • Op inc for EUC shrinking at 8-15% CAGR per BCG.[15] • Assumed op inc shrinkage of 8.2% per year results in 2023 op inc for this group of $425M, or a 2.2% op inc percentage.
Total Public Op Inc	$2,260	$3,550	4.0%	6.4%	

APPENDIX C CONTINUED

Operating Income ("Op Inc") ($M): Private Co.	2013	2023	2013 Op Inc %	2023 Op Inc %	Notes and Sources
Innovation Group	$585	$3,600	11.7%	13.3%	• 2023 op inc is set to approximately 1.5–2 percentage points lower than under public company scenario, to reflect increased R&D spend.
Enterprise Core	$675	$1,800	4.5%	5.5%	• 2023 op inc is set to about .5 percentage points lower than under public company scenario, to reflect slightly increased R&D.
Commodity Core	$1,000	$600	2.7%	2.2%	• Op inc set at same % as public company scenario. Increased R&D unlikely.
Total Private Op Inc	$2,260	$6,000	4.0%	6.9%	

Notes

INTRODUCTION

1. Johnson, Steven, *How We Got to Now: Six Innovations That Made the Modern World,* New York: Penguin Group LLC, 2014, p. 30.

2. Harte, John, *Management Crisis and Business Revolution,* New Brunswick, New Jersey: Transaction Publishers, 2014, p. 126.

ONE

1. Company annual reports.

2. Various reports and press releases from Gartner Group and International Data Corporation ("IDC").

3. Google Finance, Yahoo Finance, and Dell closing costs, 2015. Retrieved from http://www.dell.com/learn/us/en/vn/corporate-secure-en/documents-dell-closing-costs.pdf.

4. Dell annual reports and Dell closing costs, 2015. Retrieved from http://www.dell.com/learn/us/en/vn/corporate-secure-en/documents-dell-closing-costs.pdf.

5. Hester, Liz, "Dell Goes Private in Biggest LBO Since 2007," February 6, 2013. Retrieved from http://talkingbiznews.com/2/dell-goes-private-in-biggest-lbo-since-2007/.

TWO

1. Fortuna, Steven, "Compaq Reengineers the Channel: Will It Be Enough to Slow Dell's Momentum?" *Deutsche Morgan Grenfell Technology Group Research Report*, 1997, p. 6.

2. Fisher, Lawrence, "Inside Dell Computer Corporation: Managing Working Capital," 1998. Retrieved from http://www.strategy-business.com/article/9571?gko=d8c29.

3. Dell Inc., "Dell Quarterly Report 10Q for the Second Quarter of Fiscal Year 2014," 2014, p. 51.

4. IBM, "IBM Annual Report 2013," 2013, pp. 70-72.

5. Hewlett-Packard, "Hewlett-Packard 10k Report Fiscal Year 2012," 2012, p. 67.

THREE

1. Augustine, Norman (chair), *Rising Above the Gathering Storm, Revisited*, Washington, DC: The National Academies Press, 2010, p. vii.

2. Schumpeter, Joseph, *Capitalism, Socialism, and Democracy*, New York, New York: Harper & Row Publishers, Inc., 1950, pp. 81-86.

3. Augustine, Norman (chair), *Rising Above the Gathering Storm: Energizing and Employing America for a Brighter Economic Future*, Washington, DC: The National Academies Press, 2005, p. 1.

4. Augustine, Norman (chair), *Rising Above the Gathering Storm, Revisited*, Washington, DC: The National Academies Press, 2010, p. 5.

5. Ibid., pp. 6-11.

6. Hill, Linda, Brandeau, Greg, Truelove, Emily, and Lineback, Kent, *Collective Genius: The Art and Practice of Leading Innovation*, Boston, MA: Harvard Business Review Press, 2014, p. 11.

7. Christensen, Clayton, *The Innovator's Dilemma*, Boston, MA: Harvard Business School Press, 1997, p. xv.

8. Nisen, Max, "Clay Christensen: Our Obsession with Efficiency is Killing Innovation," 2012. Retrieved from http://www.businessinsider.com/clay-christensen-our-obsession-with-efficiency-is-killing-innovation-2012-12.

9. Manyika, James, Chui, Michael, Bughin, Jacques, Dobbs, Richard, Bisson, Peter, and Marrs, Alex, "Disruptive technologies: Advances that will transform life, business, and the global economy," *McKinsey & Company Research Report,* 2013, pp. 2-3.

10. Hill, Linda, Brandeau, Greg, Truelove, Emily, and Lineback, Kent, *Collective Genius: The Art and Practice of Leading Innovation*, Boston, MA: Harvard Business Review Press, 2014, p. 9.

11. "Increasing Ubiquity," 2009, par. 13. Retrieved from http://kk.org/thetechnium/increasing-ubiq/.

12. Moore, Gordon, "Cramming More Components Onto Integrated Circuits," *Proceedings of the IEEE, 86,* 1965, pp. 114-117. Retrieved from http://doi.org/10.1109/JPROC.1998.658762.

13. Brynjolfsson, Eric, and Mcafee, Andrew, *The Second Machine Age*, New York, New York: W.W. Norton & Company, Inc., 2014, pp. 49-50.

14. Ungar, Lyle. "Your iPhone is Going to Outsmart You," 2008, par. 5. Retrieved from http://scienceprogress.org/2008/05/your-iphone-is-going-to-outsmart-you/.

15. Brynjolfsson, Eric, and Mcafee, Andrew, *The Second Machine Age*, New York, New York: W.W. Norton & Company, Inc., 2014, p. 62.

16. Johnson, Steven, *How We Got to Now: Six Innovations That Made the Modern World*, New York, New York: Penguin Group LLC, pp. 14-31.

FOUR

1. McDonald, Duff, *The Firm: The Story of McKinsey*. New York, New York: Simon & Schuster, 2013, pp. 143-144.

2. Hill, Linda, Brandeau, Greg, Truelove, Emily, and Lineback, Kent, *Collective Genius: The Art and Practice of Leading Innovation*, Boston, MA: Harvard Business Review Press, 2014, pp. 45.

3. Ibid., pp. 169 and 192.

4. Brown, Tim, "Design Thinking," *Harvard Business Review,* June 2011, pp. 90-91.

5. Hill, Linda, Brandeau, Greg, Truelove, Emily, and Lineback, Kent, *Collective Genius: The Art and Practice of Leading Innovation*, Boston, MA: Harvard Business Review Press, 2014, p. 28.

6. Catmull, Ed, *Creativity, Inc.*, Toronto, Canada: Random House Canada, 2014, pp. 92-93.

7. Hill, Linda, Brandeau, Greg, Truelove, Emily, and Lineback, Kent, *Collective Genius: The Art and Practice of Leading Innovation*, Boston, MA: Harvard Business Review Press, 2014, p. 121.

8. Basadur, Tim, Gelade, Garry, and Basadur, Tim, "Creative Problem-Solving Process Styles, Cognitive Work Demands, and Organizational Adaptability," *The Journal of Applied Behavioral Science*, 50, pp. 82-83. Retrieved from http://jab.sagepub.com.ezproxy-library.ocad.ca/content/50/1/80.

full.pdf+html.

9. Tuckman, Bruce, and Jensen, Mary Ann, "Stages of Small-Group Development Revisited," *Group Facilitation*, *10*, 43–48. Retrieved from http://gom.sagepub.com.ez-proxy-library.ocad.ca/content/2/4/419.full.pdf+html.

10. Isaacson, Walter, *The Innovators*. New York, New York: Simon & Schuster, 2014, pp. 268-281.

11. Ibid., p. 275.

12. Ibid., p. 281.

13. Brown, Tim, "Design Thinking," *Harvard Business Review*, June 2011, pp. 88-89.

14. Senge, Peter, *The Fifth Discipline: The Art and Practice of the Learning Organization*. New York: Doubleday/Currency, 1990, p. 175.

15. Martin, Roger, *The Opposable Mind*, Boston, MA: Harvard Business School Publishing, 2007, p. 15.

16. Isaacson, Walter, *The Innovators*. New York, New York: Simon & Schuster, 2014, pp. 235-237.

17. Lencioni, Patrick, *The Table Group*, 2014, par. 3. Retrieved from http://www.tablegroup.com/books/dysfunctions.

18. Collins, Jim, *How the Mighty Fall*. New York, New York: Harper Collins Publishers, 2009, pp. 28-29.

19. Christensen, Clayton, *The Innovator's Solution*, Boston, MA: Harvard Business School Press, 2003, pp. 35-39.

20. Christensen, Clayton, *The Innovator's Dilemma*, Boston, MA: Harvard Business School Press, 1997, p. 91.

21. Brown, Bruce, and Anthony, Scott, "How P&G Tripled Its Innovation Success Rate," *Harvard Business Review*, June 2011, par. 20. Retrieved from https://hbr.org/2011/06/how-pg-tripled-its-innovation-success-rate.

22. Hill, Linda, Brandeau, Greg, Truelove, Emily, and Line-back, Kent, *Collective Genius: The Art and Practice of Leading Innovation*, Boston, MA: Harvard Business Review Press, 2014, p. 65.

23. Covey, Stephen, *Principle-Centered Leadership*, 1996, par. 3. Retrieved from http://www.qualitydigest.com/feb/covey.html.

24. Christensen, Clayton, *The Innovator's Solution*, Boston, MA: Harvard Business School Press, 2003, pp. 79-80.

25. Anthony, Scott, "Should Big Companies Give Up on Innovation?," March 2014, par. 12. Retrieved from http://blogs.hbr.org/2014/03/should-big-companies-give-up-on-innovation/.

26. Lev-Ram, Michael, "IBM CEO Ginni Rometty gets past the Big Blues," September 2014, par. 13. Retrieved from http://fortune.com/2014/09/18/ginni-rometty-ibm/.

27. Schumpeter, Joseph, *The Theory of Economic Development*, (Harvard University, Ed.), Cambridge, MA, 1934, p. 66.

28. Shontell, Alyson, "Here's How Long It Took 15 Hot Start-ups To Get 1,000,000 Users," 2012. Retrieved from http://www.businessinsider.com/one-million-users-startups-2012-1?op=1.

29. Johnston, David, "Idle corporate cash piles up," 2012, par. 8. Retrieved from http://blogs.reuters.com/david-cay-johnston/2012/07/16/idle-corporate-cash-piles-up/.

30. PriceWaterhouseCoopers, "MoneyTree report - historical trend data," 2014. Retrieved from https://www.pwcmoneytree.com/HistoricTrends/CustomQueryHistoricTrend.

31. Cherney, Mike, "Companies Piled On The Cash In 2013 MoneyBeat – WSJ," *The Wall Street Journal*, 2014, par. 11. Retrieved from http://blogs.wsj.com/money-beat/2014/04/14/companies-piled-on-the-cash-in-2013/.

32. Bain, "A World Awash in Money: Capital Trends Through 2020," *Bain & Company Research Report*, 2012, p. 17. Retrieved from http://www.bain.com/Images/BAIN_RE-PORT_A_world_awash_in_money.pdf.

33. Walls, Michael, and Dyer, James, "Risk Propensity and Firm Performance: A Study of the Petroleum Exploration Industry," *Management Science*, 42(7), July 1996, pp. 1004–1021. Retrieved from http://www.jstor.org.ez-proxy-library.ocad.ca/stable/pdf/2634364.pdf.

34. Howard, Ronald, "Decision Analysis: Practice and Promise," *Management Science*, Vol. 34, No. 6, June 1988, pp. 679-695. Retrieved from http://www.jstor.org.ezproxy-library.ocad.ca/stable/pdf/2632123.pdf.

35. Sutton, Robert, and Rao, Huggy, *Scaling Up Excellence*. New York: Crown Publishing Group, 2014, p. 105.

36. Collins, Jim, *How the Mighty Fall*. New York, New York: Harper Collins Publishers, 2009, p. 63 and p. 81.

37. Anthony, Scott, "Should Big Companies Give Up on Innovation?," March 2014, par. 15. Retrieved from http://blogs.hbr.org/2014/03/should-big-companies-give-up-on-innovation/.

FIVE

1. Payne, Graham, and Allen, Brandt, *Dell Computer: Business to Business Over the Web*, Charlottesville, VA: Darden Business Publishing, 1999, p. 3.

2. Haber, Lynn, "Dell PartnerDirect Summit: Dell's partner alignment shaping up," November 2014, par. 3. Retrieved from http://searchitchannel.techtarget.com/news/2240234160/Dell-PartnerDirect-Summit-Dells-partner-alignment-shaping-up.

3. Kraemer, Kenneth, and Dedrick, Jason, "Dell Computer:

Organization of a Global Production Network," University of California, Irvine, CA, 2002, par. 1. Retrieved from http://down.cenet.org.cn/upfile/47/2005131224345144. pdf.

4. Lawrentz, Heather, "Dell Releases PartnerDirect Program Updates with Channel Focus," 2013, par. 6. Retrieved from http://www.smbnation.com/content/news/entry/ dell-releases-partnerdirect-program-updates-with-channel-focus.

5. Schultz, Randall, "Compaq picks new CEO," July 1999, par. 23. Retrieved from http://money.cnn.com/1999/07/22/ technology/compaq/.

6. Forest, Stephanie, and Arnst, Catherine, "The Education Of Michael Dell," *Businessweek*, March 1993, par. 21. Retrieved from http://www.businessweek.com/stories/1993-03-21/the-education-of-michael-dell.

7. Markoff, John, "Flaw Undermines Accuracy of Pentium Chips," *The New York Times*, November 24, 1994, par. 3. Retrieved from http://www.nytimes.com/1994/11/24/business/company-news-flaw-undermines-accuracy-of-pentium-chips.html.

8. Pandya, Mukul, and Shell, Robbie, *Lasting Leadership*, Upper Saddle River, New Jersey: Wharton School Publishing, 2005, p. 6. Retrieved from https://lib.nu.edu.sa/ uploads/m1/40.pdf.

9. Markoff, John, "Flaw Undermines Accuracy of Pentium Chips," *The New York Times*, November 24, 1994, par. 1. Retrieved from http://www.nytimes.com/1994/11/24/business/company-news-flaw-undermines-accuracy-of-pentium-chips.html.

10. Emery, Vince, "The Pentium Chip Story: A Learning Experience," 1996. Retrieved from http://www.emery.com/1e/ pentium.htm.

11. Christensen, Clayton, Dyer, Jeff, and Gregersen, Hal, *The Innovator's DNA*, Boston, MA: Harvard Business School Publishing, 2011, p. 29.

SIX

1. Company reports.

2. Various reports and press releases from Gartner Group, Dataquest and IDC.

3. Noam, Eli, *Media Ownership and Concentration in America*, New York, New York: Oxford University Press, Inc., p. 194. Retrieved from https://books.google.ca/books?id=Kd_1STqyGFcC&pg=PA194&lpg=PA194.

4. Juliussen, Finn-Erik, "Worldwide PC Market," 2010, par. 3. Retrieved from http://www.etforecasts.com/products/ES_pcww1203.htm.

5. *International Comparisons of Hourly Compensation Costs in Manufacturing*, 2014. Retrieved from https://www.conference-board.org/ilcprogram/index.cfm?id=28269.

6. Lee, Louise, "Dell: Facing Up to Past Mistakes," 2006, par. 3. Retrieved from http://www.bloomberg.com/bw/stories/2006-06-18/dell-facing-up-to-past-mistakes.

7. Rivkin, Jan, "Revitalizing Dell," HBS No. 9-710-442, Boston, MA: Harvard Business School Publishing, 2010, p. 13.

8. Google Finance, Yahoo Finance, and Dell closing costs, 2015. Retrieved from http://www.dell.com/learn/us/en/vn/corporate-secure-en/documents-dell-closing-costs.pdf.

9. Huey, John, "How McKinsey Does It," *Fortune*, November 1, 1993. Retrieved from http://archive.fortune.com/magazines/fortune/fortune_archive/1993/11/01/78550/index.htm.

10. Martin, Roger, "Two Words That Kill Innovation," *Harvard Business Review,* December 9, 2014, par. 2. Retrieved from https://hbr.org/2014/12/two-words-that-kill-innovation.

11. Ames, Ben, "Dell E-Mail Details Corporate Reforms," *ITWorld Canada*, February 5, 2007, par. 4. Retrieved from http://www.itworldcanada.com/article/michael-dell-says-new-smb-focus-will-turn-around-the-company/5571.

12. Strumpf, Dan, "U.S. Public Companies Rise Again," *The Wall Street Journal*, February 5, 2014, par. 2. Retrieved from http://www.wsj.com/articles/SB1000142405270230485110457936327210717430.

13. Dell closing costs, 2015. Retrieved from http://www.dell.com/learn/us/en/vn/corporate-secure-en/documents-dell-closing-costs.pdf.

14. Yahoo Finance, 2015.

15. Ferreira, Daniel, Silva, Andre, & Manso, Gustavo, "Incentives to Innovate and the Decision to Go Public or Private," London School of Economics, 2012, p.288. Retrieved from http://rfs.oxfordjournals.org.ezproxy-library.ocad.ca/content/27/1/256.full.pdf+html.

SEVEN

1. McCabe, Laurie, "Nine Signs Michael Dell Will Be the Comeback Kid," 2014, par. 11. Retrieved from http://

lauriemccabe.com/2014/06/10/nine-signs-michael-dell-will-be-the-comeback-kid/.

2. Kavanaugh, Kelly, "Magic Quadrant for Global MSSPs," *Gartner Group Research Report*, 2014, p. 2. Retrieved from http://www.secureworks.com/assets/pdf-store/other/gartner.mq.global.mssp.2014.pdf.

3. Pezzini, Massimo, Natis, Yefim, Malinverno, Paolo, Iijima, Kimihiko, Thompson, Jess, Thoo, Eric, Guttridge, Keith, "Magic Quadrant for Enterprise Integration Platform as a Service," *Gartner Group Research Report*, 2015. Retrieved from http://www.gartner.com/technology/reprints.do?id=1-2C8JHQO&ct=150325&st=sg.

4. Burt, Jeffrey, "Dell Sets Different Cloud Path Than HP, IBM," 2013, par. 1, 4, 6. Retrieved from http://www.eweek.com/cloud/dell-sets-different-cloud-path-than-hp-ibm.html.

5. Macomber, Krista, "Dell's Hardware Revenue Continues to Grow, but Further Gains Will Depend on a Faster Go-to-Market Transformation," 2014, par. 10. Retrieved from http://www.computer.org/web/computingnow/insights/content?g=53319&type=article&urlTitle=dell%E2%80%99s-hardware-revenue-continues-to-grow-but-further-gains-will-depend-on-a-faster-go-to-market-transformation.

6. Kelly, Jeff, "Big Data Revenue and Market Forecast 2012-2017," 2013, par. 7. Retrieved from http://wikibon.org/wiki/v/Big_Data_Vendor_Revenue_and_Market_Forecast_2012-2017#Big_Data_Vendor_Revenue.

7. Ubrani, Jitesh, "Worldwide Tablet Shipments Miss Target as First Quarter Experiences Single-Digit Growth," *IDC Research Report*, 2014, par. 5. Retrieved from http://www.idc.com/getdoc.jsp?containerId=prUS24833314.

8. Bourne, James, "HP tops IDC Cloud Infrastructure Market Rankings, ahead of Dell and Cisco,"2015, par. 2. Retrieved from http://www.cloudcomputing-news. net/news/2015/jul/03/hp-tops-idc-cloud-infrastructure-market-rankings-ahead-dell-and-cisco/.

9. Kitagawa, Mikako, "Gartner Says Worldwide PC Shipments in the Third Quarter of 2014 Declined .5 Percent," *IDC Research Report*, 2014, par. 6. Retrieved from http://www.gartner.com/newsroom/id/2869019.

10. Gagliordi, Natalie, "Dell Secureworks Launches Threat Detection Managed Service," 2014, par. 8. Retrieved from http://www.zdnet.com/article/dell-secureworks-launches-threat-detection-managed-service/.

11. Bhas, Nitin, "Smart Wearable Devices," *Juniper Research Ltd. Report*, 2013, p.16.

12. Yarow, Jay, "Apple's iWatch Could Be Super Profitable for Apple," 2013, par. 5. Retrieved from http://www. businessinsider.com/apples-iwatch-could-be-super-profitable-for-apple-2013-3.

13. Moorhead, Patrick, "HP and IBM Need to Be Very Afraid of Dell," *Forbes*, 2012, par. 4. Retrieved from http://www. forbes.com/sites/patrickmoorhead/2012/04/30/hp-and-ibm-need-to-be-very-afraid-of-dell/.

14. Fortt, Jon, "Michael Dell on the state of PCs and going private," 2014, par. 16. Retrieved from http://www.cnbc. com/id/102026551.

15. Haber, Lynn, "Dell PartnerDirect Summit: Dell's Partner Alignment Shaping Up," 2014, par. 1. Retrieved from http://searchitchannel.techtarget.com/news/2240234160/ Dell-PartnerDirect-Summit-Dells-partner-alignment-shaping-up.

16. Bernstein, Shai, "Does Going Public Affect Innovation?" Stanford University, 2014, p. 3. Retrieved from https://www.gsb.stanford.edu/sites/gsb/files/publication-pdf/IPOInnovation July2014.pdf.

17. Hsu, David, and Aggarwal, Vikas, "Entrepreneurial Exits and Innovation," INSEAD, 2013, pp. 24-25. Retrieved from http://www.insead.edu/facultyresearch/research/doc.cfm?did=52807.

18. Aggarwal, Vikas, and Kessler, Ben, "Preserving Innovation Flair," INSEAD, 2013, par. 8. Retrieved from http://knowledge.insead.edu/leadership-management/strategy/preserving-innovation-flair-2598.

19. Ferreira, Daniel, Silva, Andre, and Manso, Gustavo, "Incentives to Innovate and the Decision to Go Public or Private," London School of Economics, 2012, p.288. Retrieved from http://rfs.oxfordjournals.org.ezproxy-library.ocad.ca/content/27/1/256.full.pdf+html.

20. Collis, David, Yoffie, David, and Shaffer, Matthew, "Taking Dell Private," HBS No. 9-714-421, Boston, MA: Harvard Business School Publishing, 2013, pp. 10-36.

21. Boston Consulting Group, "Project Denali," Boston, 2013, p. 9 and p. 11. Retrieved from http://www.sec.gov/Archives/edgar/data/826083/000119312513134593/d505474dex99c15.htm.

22. J.P. Morgan, "Presentation to the Denali Board of Directors," New York, 2013, p. 10 and p. 12. Retrieved from http://www.sec.gov/Archives/edgar/data/826083/000119312513134593/d505474dex99c5.htm.

23. Boston Consulting Group, "Project Denali," Boston, 2013, p. 11. Retrieved from http://www.sec.gov/Archives/edgar/data/826083/000119312513134593/d505474dex99c15.htm.

24. Dell Inc., "Dell Quarterly Report 10Q for the Second Quarter of Fiscal Year 2014," Austin, Texas, 2013, p. 30. Retrieved from http://www.sec.gov/Archives/edgar/data/826083/000082608313000028/dellq2fy1410q.htm.

25. Dell Inc., "Dell 10k Fiscal Year 2013," Austin, Texas, 2013, pp. 50-52. Retrieved from http://www.sec.gov/Archives/edgar/data/826083/000082608313000005/dellfy1310k.htm.

26. J.P. Morgan, "Presentation to the Denali Board of Directors," New York, 2013, p. 12. Retrieved from http://www.sec.gov/Archives/edgar/data/826083/000119312513134593/d505474dex99c5.htm.

27. Dell Inc, "State and Future of Dell's Channel Business," 2013, p. 5. Retrieved from http://www.slideshare.net/Dell/state-and-future-of-dells-channel-business-36302979.

28. Verrastro, Justin, "Report: Managed Security Services to Boast 15.4% CAGR Between 2013 and 2019," 2014, par. 2. Retrieved from http://www.apextechservices.com/topics/articles/386238-report-managed-security-services-boast-154-cagr-between.htm.

29. Sommer, Dan, "Gartner Says Worldwide Business Intelligence and Analytics Software Market Grew 8 Percent in 2013," 2014, par. 1. Retrieved from http://www.gartner.com/newsroom/id/2723717.

30. Golson, Jordan, "Apple Reports Q4 2014 Year-End

Results: $8.5 Billion Profit on $42.1 Billion in Revenue," 2014, par. 3. Retrieved from http://www.macrumors. com/2014/10/20/apple-earnings-fiscal-2014/.

31. Nixon, David, "Top 25 Largest Private Companies in 2013," 2014, p. 24. Retrieved March 19, 2015, from http://www.insidermonkey.com/blog/top-25-largest-private-companies-in-2013-in-the-us-314440/.

32. Dell Inc., "Dell 10k Fiscal Year 2013," Austin, Texas, 2013, p. 3. Retrieved from http://www.sec.gov/Archives/edgar/data/826083/000082608313000005/dellfy1310k.htm.

33. Carey, David, and Clark, Jack, "Dell, Silver Lake Said to Reap 90% Gain a Year After LBO," *Bloomberg Business,* November 6, 2014, par. 2 and 3. Retrieved from http://www.bloomberg.com/news/articles/2014-11-06/dell-silver-lake-said-to-reap-90-gain-a-year-after-lbo.

34. Ibid., par. 1 and 8.

35. "Dell Upgraded by S&P as It Chips Away at Its Debt," *fastFT,* 2014, par. 2 and 8. Retrieved from http://www.ft.com/fastft/246411/dell-upgraded-bb-sandp.

36. Carey, David, and Clark, Jack, "Dell, Silver Lake Said to Reap 90% Gain a Year After LBO," *Bloomberg Business,* November 6, 2014, par. 2. Retrieved from http://www.bloomberg.com/news/articles/2014-11-06/dell-silver-lake-said-to-reap-90-gain-a-year-after-lbo.

37. McCarron, Catriona, "Private Equity-Backed Portfolio Company Holding Periods," *Private Equity Spotlight,* April 2014. Retrieved from https://www.preqin.com/docs/newsletters/pe/Preqin_PESL_May_14_PE_Holding_Periods.pdf.

38. Forrest, Conner, "The 10 Largest Tech Acquisitions of All Time," August 2014. Retrieved from http://www.techrepublic.com/article/the-10-largest-tech-acquisitions-of-all-time/.

EIGHT

1. White, Anthony, "Urban Dictionary: freak flag," 2006. Retrieved from http://www.urbandictionary.com/define.php?term=freak+flag.

2. Sutton, Robert, and Rao, Huggy, *Scaling Up Excellence,* New York: Crown Publishing Group, 2014, p. 6.

3. Dell Inc., "Dell Quarterly Report 10Q for the Second Quarter of Fiscal Year 2014," Austin, Texas, 2013, p. 41. Retrieved from http://www.sec.gov/Archives/edgar/data/826083/000082608313000028/dellq2fy1410q.htm.

APPENDIX A

1. Porter, Michael, *Competitive Strategy: Techniques for Analyzing Industries and Competitors,* New York: Free Press, 1980, p. 4. (Republished with a new introduction, 1998.)

2. NTT, "NTT Positioned as a 'Challenger' in the Gartner Magic Quadrant for Global Managed Security Service Providers," 2014, par. 6. Retrieved from http://www.marketwired.com/press-release/ntt-positioned-as-challenger-gartner-magic-quadrant-global-managed-security-service-nyse-ntt-1889307.htm.

3. James, Daniel, "Opportunities in Security Software," 2013, par. 6. Retrieved from http://www.fool.com/investing/general/2013/08/21/opportunities-in-security-

software.aspx.

4. Kavanaugh, Kelly, "Magic Quadrant for Global MSSPs," *Gartner Group Research Report,* 2014, par. 5. Retrieved from http://www.secureworks.com/assets/pdf-store/other/gartner.mq.global.mssp.2014.pdf.

5. Sommer, Dan, "Gartner Says Worldwide Business Intelligence and Analytics Software Market Grew 8 Percent in 2013," 2014, par. 1. Retrieved from http://www.gartner.com/newsroom/id/2723717.

6. Alessi, "SAP Drops Margin Forecast, Posts Fall in Profit," *The Wall Street Journal*, 2015, par. 8. Retrieved from http://www.wsj.com/articles/sap-profit-hurt-in-shift-to-cloud-based-products-1421738065.

7. Columbus, Louis, "Key Take-Aways From Gartner's 2015 Magic Quadrant For Business Intelligence And Analytics Platforms," *Forbes*, 2015, par. 4. Retrieved from http://www.forbes.com/sites/louiscolumbus/2015/02/25/key-take-aways-from-gartners-2015-magic-quadrant-for-business-intelligence-and-analytics-platforms/.

8. Columbus, Louis, "Gartner Predicts Infrastructure Services Will Accelerate Cloud Computing Growth," *Forbes,* 2013, par. 2 and 3. Retrieved from http://www.forbes.com/sites/louiscolumbus/2013/02/19/gartner-predicts-infrastructure-services-will-accelerate-cloud-computing-growth/.

9. Gaudin, Sharon, "Enterprises Increasingly Look to the Private Cloud," *Computerworld,* 2014, par. 4. Retrieved from http://www.computerworld.com/article/2490138/private-cloud/enterprises-increasingly-look-to-the-private-cloud.html.

10. Van der Meulen, Rob, and Rivera, Janessa, "Gartner Says Worldwide IT Spending on Pace to Grow 2.4 Percent in 2015," *Gartner Group Research Report,* 2015, par. 4. Retrieved from http://www.gartner.com/newsroom/id/2959717.

11. Gottfried, Miriam, "HEARD ON THE STREET: Reaching for the Cloud Could Lift Amazon's Margins Off the Ground," *The Wall Street Journal*, 2013, par. 9. Retrieved from http://www.wsj.com/articles/SB100014241 27887324442304578236000008569908.

12. Maurer, William, Ackerman, David, and Britz, Bryan, "Magic Quadrant for Data Center Outsourcing and Infrastructure Utility Services, North America," *Gartner Group Research Report,* 2014, par. 8. Retrieved from http://www.gartner.com/technology/reprints.do?id=1-1YJLNPF&ct=140731&st=sb.

13. "The State of the Tablet Market," *TabTimes*, 2015. Retrieved from http://tabtimes.com/resources/the-state-of-the-tablet-market/.

14. "Biggest tablet profit margins: Microsoft, Apple," *USA Today*, 2012, par. 9. Retrieved from http://www.usatoday.com/story/tech/2012/11/05/microsoft-apple-tablets-have-most-profit-margins/1684863/.

15. Reader, Ruth, "IDC: Tablet Shipments Decline for the First Time in Q4 2014," 2015, par. 5. Retrieved from http://venturebeat.com/2015/02/02/idc-tablet-shipments-decline-for-the-first-time-in-q4-2014-leaders-apple-and-samsung-both-lose-market-share/.

16. Kitagawa, Mikako, "Gartner Says PC Shipments Grew 1 Percent in Fourth Quarter of 2014," *Gartner Group Research Report,* 2015, par. 14. Retrieved from http://

www.gartner.com/newsroom/id/2960125.

17. Arthur, Charles, "How the "Value Trap" Squeezes Windows PC Makers' Revenues and Profits", *The Guardian,* 2014, par. 9 and 16. Retrieved from http://www.theguardian.com/technology/2014/jan/09/pc-value-trap-windows-chrome-hp-dell-lenovo-asus-acer.

APPENDIX B

1. Bort, Julie, "Dell's $600 Million Acquisition of Wyse is Another Boneheaded Move," 2012. Retrieved from http://www.businessinsider.com/buying-wyse-could-be-dells-latest-bonehead-move-2012-4.

APPENDIX C

1. Dell Inc., "Dell 10k Fiscal Year 2013," Austin, Texas, 2013, p. 39. Retrieved from http://www.sec.gov/Archives/edgar/data/826083/000082608313000005/dellfy1310k.htm.

2. Boston Consulting Group, "Project Denali," Boston, 2013, p. 9. Retrieved from http://www.sec.gov/Archives/edgar/data/826083/000119312513134593/d505474dex99c15.htm.

3. Sommer, Dan, "Gartner Says Worldwide Business Intelligence and Analytics Software Market Grew 8 Percent in 2013," 2014, par. 1. Retrieved from http://www.gartner.com/newsroom/id/2723717.

4. NTT, "NTT Positioned as a 'Challenger' in the Gartner Magic Quadrant for Global Managed Security Service Providers," 2014, par. 6. Retrieved from http://www.marketwired.com/press-release/ntt-positioned-as-challenger-gartner-magic-quadrant-global-managed-

security-service-nyse-ntt-1889307.htm.

5. Columbus, Louis, "Gartner Predicts Infrastructure Services Will Accelerate Cloud Computing Growth," *Forbes,* 2013, par. 2. Retrieved from http://www.forbes. com/sites/louiscolumbus/2013/02/19/gartner-predicts-infrastructure-services-will-accelerate-cloud-computing-growth/.

6. J.P. Morgan, "Presentation to the Denali Board of Directors," New York, 2013, p. 10. Retrieved from http://www.sec.gov/Archives/edgar/data/826083/000119312513134593/d505474dex99c5. htm.

7. Boston Consulting Group, "Project Denali," Boston, 2013, p. 11. Retrieved from http://www.sec.gov/Archives/edgar/data/826083/000119312513134593/d505474dex99c15. htm.

8. Schatzker, Erik, "Michael Dell: 10+ Companies Have Asked for Advice on Going Private," 2014, p. 3. Retrieved from http://www.valuewalk.com/2014/12/michael-dell-10-companies-asked-advice-going-private/.

9. Eastwood, Matt, and Stolarski, Kuba, "Worldwide Server Market Revenues Increase 1.9% in the Fourth Quarter," IDC press release, 2015, par. 6. Retrieved from http://www.idc.com/getdoc.jsp?containerId=prUS25461815.

10. Chanthadavong, Aimee, "Dell Celebrates First Year of Freedom with Growth," *ZDNet,* 2014, par. 3. Retrieved from http://www.zdnet.com/article/dell-celebrates-first-year-of-freedom-with-growth/.

11. Loverde, Loren, "PC Leaders Continue Growth and Share Gains as Market Remains Slow," IDC press release,

2015, par. 6. Retrieved from http://www.idc.com/getdoc. jsp?containerId=prUS25372415.

12. Statista, "Average Selling Prices of Desktop PCs Worldwide," 2015. Retrieved from http://www.statista. com/statistics/203759/average-selling-price-of-desktop-pcs-worldwide/.

13. Dell Inc., "Dell 10k Fiscal Year 2013," Austin, Texas, 2013, p. 52. Retrieved from http://www.sec.gov/Archives/ edgar/data/826083/000082608313000005/dellfy1310k. htm.

14. Dell Inc., "Dell 10k Fiscal Year 2013," Austin, Texas, 2013, p. 51. Retrieved from http://www.sec.gov/Archives/ edgar/data/826083/000082608313000005/dellfy1310k. htm.

15. Dell Special Committee, *Dell Special Committee Investor Presentation*, Austin, Texas, 2013, p. 18. Retrieved from http://www.sec.gov/Archives/edgar/ data/826083/000119312513247883/d550356ddefa14a. htm.

16. Dell Inc., "Dell 10k Fiscal Year 2013," Austin, Texas, 2013, p. 50. Retrieved from http://www.sec.gov/Archives/ edgar/data/826083/000082608313000005/dellfy1310k. htm.

Bibliography

Aggarwal, Vikas, and Kessler, Ben, "Preserving Innovation Flair," INSEAD, 2013. Retrieved from http://knowledge.insead.edu/leadership-management/strategy/preserving-innovation-flair-2598.

Alessi, "SAP Drops Margin Forecast, Posts Fall in Profit," *The Wall Street Journal*, 2015. Retrieved from http://www.wsj.com/articles/sap-profit-hurt-in-shift-to-cloud-based-products-1421738065.

Ames, Ben, "Dell E-Mail Details Corporate Reforms," *ITWorld Canada*, February 5, 2007. Retrieved from http://www.itworldcanada.com/article/michael-dell-says-new-smb-focus-will-turn-around-the-company/5571.

Anthony, Scott, "Should Big Companies Give Up on Innovation?," March 2014. Retrieved from http://blogs.hbr.org/2014/03/should-big-companies-give-up-on-innovation/.

Arthur, Charles, "How the "Value Trap" Squeezes Windows PC Makers' Revenues and Profits", *The Guardian*, 2014. Retrieved from http://www.theguardian.com/technology/2014/jan/09/pc-value-trap-windows-chrome-hp-dell-lenovo-asus-acer.

Augustine, Norman (chair), *Rising Above the Gathering Storm: Energizing and Employing America for a Brighter Economic Future,* Washington, DC: The National Academies Press, 2005.

Augustine, Norman (chair), *Rising Above the Gathering Storm, Revisited,* Washington, DC: The National Academies Press, 2010.

Bain, "A World Awash in Money: Capital Trends Through 2020," *Bain & Company Research Report,* 2012. Retrieved from http://www.bain.com/Images/BAIN_REPORT_A_world_awash_in_money.pdf.

Basadur, Tim, Gelade, Garry, and Basadur, Tim, "Creative Problem-Solving Process Styles, Cognitive Work Demands, and Organizational Adaptability," *The Journal of Applied Behavioral Science.* Retrieved from http://jab.sagepub.com.ezproxy-library.ocad.ca/content/50/1/80.full.pdf+html.

Bernstein, Shai, "Does Going Public Affect Innovation?" Stanford University, 2014. Retrieved from https://www.gsb.stanford.edu/sites/gsb/files/publication-pdf/IPOInnovationJuly2014.pdf.

Bhas, Nitin, "Smart Wearable Devices," *Juniper Research Ltd. Report,* 2013.

"Biggest Tablet Profit Margins: Microsoft, Apple," *USA Today,* 2012. Retrieved from http://www.usatoday.com/story/tech/2012/11/05/microsoft-apple-tablets-have-most-profit-margins/1684863/.

Bort, Julie, "Dell's $600 Million Acquisition of Wyse is Another Boneheaded Move," 2012. Retrieved from http://www.businessinsider.com/buying-wyse-could-be-dells-latest-bonehead-move-2012-4.

Boston Consulting Group, "Project Denali," Boston, 2013. Retrieved from http://www.sec.gov/Archives/edgar/data/826083/000119312513134593/d505474dex99c15.

htm.

Bourne, James, "HP tops IDC Cloud Infrastructure Market Rankings, Ahead of Dell and Cisco," 2015. Retrieved from http://www.cloudcomputing-news.net/news/2015/jul/03/hp-tops-idc-cloud-infrastructure-market-rankings-ahead-dell-and-cisco/.

Brown, Bruce, and Anthony, Scott, "How P&G Tripled Its Innovation Success Rate," *Harvard Business Review*, June 2011. Retrieved from https://hbr.org/2011/06/how-pg-tripled-its-innovation-success-rate.

Brown, Tim, "Design Thinking," *Harvard Business Review,* June 2011.

Brynjolfsson, Eric, and Mcafee, Andrew, *The Second Machine Age,* New York, NY: W.W. Norton & Company, Inc., 2014.

Burt, Jeffrey, "Dell Sets Different Cloud Path Than HP, IBM," 2013. Retrieved from http://www.eweek.com/cloud/dell-sets-different-cloud-path-than-hp-ibm.html.

Carey, David, and Clark, Jack, "Dell, Silver Lake Said to Reap 90% Gain a Year After LBO," *Bloomberg Business,* November 6, 2014. Retrieved from http://www.bloomberg.com/news/articles/2014-11-06/dell-silver-lake-said-to-reap-90-gain-a-year-after-lbo.

Catmull, Ed, *Creativity, Inc.*, Toronto, Canada: Random House Canada, 2014.

Chanthadavong, Aimee, "Dell Celebrates First Year of Freedom with Growth," *ZDNet,* 2014. Retrieved from http://www.zdnet.com/article/dell-celebrates-first-year-of-freedom-with-growth/.

Cherney, Mike, "Companies Piled On The Cash In 2013 MoneyBeat – WSJ," *The Wall Street Journal,* 2014. Retrieved from http://blogs.wsj.com/moneybeat/2014/04/14/companies-piled-on-the-cash-in-2013/.

Christensen, Clayton, *The Innovator's Dilemma*, Boston, MA: Harvard Business School Press, 1997.

Christensen, Clayton, *The Innovator's Solution*, Boston, MA: Harvard Business School Press, 2003.

Christensen, Clayton, Dyer, Jeff, and Gregersen, Hal, *The Innovator's DNA*, Boston, MA: Harvard Business School Publishing, 2011.

Collins, Jim, *How the Mighty Fall*. New York, NY: Harper Collins Publishers, 2009.

Collis, David, Yoffie, David, and Shaffer, Matthew, "Taking Dell Private," HBS No. 9-714-421, Boston, Massachusetts: Harvard Business School Publishing, 2013.

Columbus, Louis, "Gartner Predicts Infrastructure Services Will Accelerate Cloud Computing Growth," *Forbes*, 2013. Retrieved from http://www.forbes.com/sites/louiscolumbus/2013/02/19/gartner-predicts-infrastructure-services-will-accelerate-cloud-computing-growth/.

Columbus, Louis, "Key Take-Aways From Gartner's 2015 Magic Quadrant for Business Intelligence And Analytics Platforms," *Forbes*, 2015. Retrieved from http://www.forbes.com/sites/louiscolumbus/2015/02/25/key-take-aways-from-gartners-2015-magic-quadrant-for-business-intelligence-and-analytics-platforms/.

Covey, Stephen, *Principle-Centered Leadership*, 1996. Retrieved from http://www.qualitydigest.com/feb/covey.html.

Dell closing costs, 2015. Retrieved from http://www.dell.com/learn/us/en/vn/corporate-secure-en/documents-dell-closing-costs.pdf.

Dell Inc., "Dell 10k Fiscal Year 2013," Austin, Texas, 2013. Retrieved from http://www.sec.gov/Archives/edgar/data/826083/000082608313000005/dellfy1310k.htm.

Dell Inc., "Dell Quarterly Report 10Q for the Second

Quarter of Fiscal Year 2014," Austin, Texas, 2013. Retrieved from http://www.sec.gov/Archives/edgar/data/826083/000082608313000028/dellq2fy1410q.htm.

Dell Inc., "State and Future of Dell's Channel Business," 2013. Retrieved from http://www.slideshare.net/Dell/state-and-future-of-dells-channel-business-36302979.

Dell Special Committee, *Dell Special Committee Investor Presentation*, Austin, Texas, 2013. Retrieved from http://www.sec.gov/Archives/edgar/data/826083/000119312513247883/d550356ddefa14a.htm.

"Dell Upgraded by S&P as It Chips Away at Its Debt," *fastFT*, 2014. Retrieved from http://www.ft.com/fastft/246411/dell-upgraded-bb-sandp.

Eastwood, Matt, and Stolarski, Kuba, "Worldwide Server Market Revenues Increase 1.9% in the Fourth Quarter," *IDC press release*, 2015. Retrieved from http://www.idc.com/getdoc.jsp?containerId=prUS25461815.

Emery, Vince, "The Pentium Chip Story: A Learning Experience", 1996. Retrieved from http://www.emery.com/1e/pentium.htm.

Ferreira, Daniel, Silva, Andre, and Manso, Gustavo, "Incentives to Innovate and the Decision to Go Public or Private," London School of Economics, 2012. Retrieved from http://rfs.oxfordjournals.org.ezproxy-library.ocad.ca/content/27/1/256.full.pdf+html.

Fisher, Lawrence, "Inside Dell Computer Corporation: Managing Working Capital," 1998. Retrieved from http://www.strategy-business.com/article/9571?gko=d8c29.

Forest, Stephanie, and Arnst, Catherine, "The Education of Michael Dell," *Businessweek*, March 1993. Retrieved from http://www.businessweek.com/stories/1993-03-21/the-education-of-michael-dell.

Forrest, Conner, "The 10 Largest Tech Acquisitions of All Time," August 2014. Retrieved from http://www.techrepublic.com/article/the-10-largest-tech-acquisitions-of-all-time/.

Fortt, Jon, "Michael Dell on the State of PCs and Going Private," 2014. Retrieved from http://www.cnbc.com/id/102026551.

Fortuna, Steven, "Compaq Reengineers the Channel: Will it Be Enough to Slow Dell's Momentum?" *Deutsche Morgan Grenfell Technology Group Research Report*, 1997.

Gagliordi, Natalie, "Dell Secureworks Launches Threat Detection Managed Service," 2014. Retrieved from http://www.zdnet.com/article/dell-secureworks-launches-threat-detection-managed-service/.

Gaudin, Sharon, "Enterprises Increasingly Look to the Private Cloud," *Computerworld*, 2014. Retrieved from http://www.computerworld.com/article/2490138/private-cloud/enterprises-increasingly-look-to-the-private-cloud.html.

Golson, Jordan, "Apple Reports Q4 2014 Year-End Results: $8.5 Billion Profit on $42.1 Billion in Revenue," 2014. Retrieved from http://www.macrumors.com/2014/10/20/apple-earnings-fiscal-2014/.

Gottfried, Miriam, "HEARD ON THE STREET: Reaching for the Cloud Could Lift Amazon's Margins Off the Ground," *The Wall Street Journal,* 2013. Retrieved from http://www.wsj.com/articles/SB10001424127887324442304578236000008569908.

Haber, Lynn, "Dell PartnerDirect Summit: Dell's partner alignment shaping up," November 2014. Retrieved from http://searchitchannel.techtarget.com/news/2240234160/Dell-PartnerDirect-Summit-Dells-partner-alignment-shaping-up.

Harte, John, *Management Crisis and Business Revolution.* New Brunswick, New Jersey: Transaction Publishers, 2014.

Hester, Liz, "Dell goes private in biggest LBO since 2007," February 6, 2013. Retrieved from http://talkingbiznews. com/2/dell-goes-private-in-biggest-lbo-since-2007/.

Hewlett-Packard, "Hewlett-Packard 10k Report Fiscal Year 2012," 2012.

Hill, Linda, Brandeau, Greg, Truelove, Emily, and Lineback, Kent, *Collective Genius: The Art and Practice of Leading Innovation,* Boston, MA: Harvard Business Review Press, 2014.

Howard, Ronald, "Decision Analysis: Practice and Promise," *Management Science,* Vol. 34, No. 6, June 1988. Retrieved from http://www.jstor.org.ezproxy-library.ocad.ca/stable/ pdf/2632123.pdf.

Hsu, David, and Aggarwal, Vikas, "Entrepreneurial Exits and Innovation," INSEAD, 2013. Retrieved from http://www. insead.edu/facultyresearch/research/doc.cfm?did=52807.

Huey, John, "How McKinsey Does It," *Fortune,* November 1, 1993. Retrieved from http://archive.fortune.com/mag-azines/fortune/fortune_archive/1993/11/01/78550/index. htm.

IBM, "IBM Annual Report 2013," 2013.

"Increasing Ubiquity," 2009. Retrieved from http://kk.org/the-technium/increasing-ubiq/.

International Comparisons of Hourly Compensation Costs in Manufacturing, 2014. Retrieved from https://www.confer-ence-board.org/ilcprogram/index.cfm?id=28269.

Isaacson, Walter, *The Innovators.* New York, New York: Si-mon & Schuster, 2014.

James, Daniel, "Opportunities in Security Software," 2013. Retrieved from http://www.fool.com/investing/general/2013/08/21/opportunities-in-security-software.aspx.

Johnson, Steven, *How We Got to Now: Six Innovations That Made the Modern World.* New York: Penguin Group LLC, 2014.

Johnston, David, "Idle Corporate Cash Piles Up," 2012. Retrieved from http://blogs.reuters.com/david-cay-johnston/2012/07/16/idle-corporate-cash-piles-up/.

Juliussen, Finn-Erik, "Worldwide PC Market," 2010. Retrieved from http://www.etforecasts.com/products/ES_pcww1203.htm.

Kavanaugh, Kelly, "Magic Quadrant for Global MSSPs," *Gartner Group Research Report,* 2014. Retrieved from http://www.secureworks.com/assets/pdf-store/other/gartner.mq.global.mssp.2014.pdf.

Kelly, Jeff, "Big Data Revenue and Market Forecast 2012-2017," 2013. Retrieved from http://wikibon.org/wiki/v/Big_Data_Vendor_Revenue_and_Market_Forecast_2012-2017#Big_Data_Vendor_Revenue.

Kitagawa, Mikako, "Gartner Says PC Shipments Grew 1 Percent in Fourth Quarter of 2014," *Gartner Group Research Report,* 2015. Retrieved from http://www.gartner.com/newsroom/id/2960125.

Kitagawa, Mikako, "Gartner Says Worldwide PC Shipments in the Third Quarter of 2014 Declined .5 Percent," *IDC Research Report,* 2014. Retrieved from http://www.gartner.com/newsroom/id/2869019.

Kraemer, Kenneth, and Dedrick, Jason, "Dell Computer: Organization of a Global Production Network," University of California, Irvine, CA, 2002. Retrieved from http://down.cenet.org.cn/upfile/47/2005131224345144.pdf.

Lawrentz, Heather, "Dell Releases PartnerDirect Program Updates with Channel Focus," 2013. Retrieved from http://www.smbnation.com/content/news/entry/dell-releases-partnerdirect-program-updates-with-channel-focus.

Lee, Louise, "Dell: Facing Up to Past Mistakes," 2006. Retrieved from http://www.bloomberg.com/bw/stories/2006-06-18/dell-facing-up-to-past-mistakes.

Lencioni, Patrick, *The Table Group*, 2014. Retrieved from http://www.tablegroup.com/books/dysfunctions.

Lev-Ram, Michael, "IBM CEO Ginni Rometty Gets Past the Big Blues," September 2014. Retrieved from http://fortune.com/2014/09/18/ginni-rometty-ibm/.

Loverde, Loren, "PC Leaders Continue Growth and Share Gains as Market Remains Slow," *IDC press release*, 2015. Retrieved from http://www.idc.com/getdoc.jsp?containerId=prUS25372415.

Macomber, Krista, "Dell's Hardware Revenue Continues to Grow, but Further Gains Will Depend on a Faster Go-To Market Transformation," 2014. Retrieved from http://www.computer.org/web/computingnow/insights/co nten t?g=53319&type=article&urlTitle=dell%E2%80%99s-hardware-revenue-continues-to-grow-but-further-gainswill-depend-on-a-faster-go-to-market-transformation.

Manyika, James, Chui, Michael, Bughin, Jacques, Dobbs, Richard, Bisson, Peter, and Marrs, Alex, "Disruptive Technologies: Advances That Will Transform Life, Business, and the Global Economy," *McKinsey & Company Research Report*, 2013.

Markoff, John, "Flaw Undermines Accuracy of Pentium Chips," *The New York Times*, November 24, 1994. Retrieved from http://www.nytimes.com/1994/11/24/business/company-news-flaw-undermines-accuracy-of-pentium-chips.html.

Martin, Roger, *The Opposable Mind*, Boston, MA: Harvard Business School Publishing.

Martin, Roger, "Two Words That Kill Innovation," *Harvard Business Review,* December 9, 2014. Retrieved from https://hbr.org/2014/12/two-words-that-kill-innovation.

Maurer, William, Ackerman, David, & Britz, Bryan, "Magic Quadrant for Data Center Outsourcing and Infrastructure Utility Services, North America," *Gartner Group Research Report,* 2014. Retrieved from http://www.gartner.com/technology/reprints.do?id=1-1YJLNPF&ct=140731&st=sb.

McCabe, Laurie, "Nine Signs Michael Dell Will Be the Comeback Kid," 2014. Retrieved from http://lauriemccabe.com/2014/06/10/nine-signs-michael-dell-will-be-the-comeback-kid/.

McCarron, Catriona, "Private Equity-Backed Portfolio Company Holding Periods," *Private Equity Spotlight,* April 2014. Retrieved from https://www.preqin.com/docs/newsletters/pe/Preqin_PESL_May_14_PE_Holding_Periods.pdf.

McDonald, Duff, *The Firm: The Story of McKinsey*. New York, NY: Simon & Schuster, 2013.

Moore, Gordon, "Cramming More Components Onto Integrated Circuits," *Proceedings of the IEEE, 86,* 1965. Retrieved from http://doi.org/10.1109/JPROC.1998.658762.

Moorhead, Patrick, "HP and IBM Need to Be Very Afraid of Dell," *Forbes,* 2012. Retrieved from http://www.forbes.com/sites/patrickmoorhead/2012/04/30/hp-and-ibm-need-to-be-very-afraid-of-dell/.

J.P. Morgan, "Presentation to the Denali Board of Directors," New York, 2013. Retrieved from http://www.sec.gov/Archives/edgar/data/826083/000119312513134593/d505474dex99c5.htm.

Nisen, Max, "Clay Christensen: Our Obsession with Efficiency is Killing Innovation," 2012. Retrieved from http://www.businessinsider.com/clay-christensen-our-obsession-with-efficiency-is-killing-innovation-2012-12.

Nixon, David, "Top 25 Largest Private Companies in 2013," 2014. Retrieved March 19, 2015, from http://www.insidermonkey.com/blog/top-25-largest-private-companies-in-2013-in-the-us-314440/.

Noam, Eli, *Media Ownership and Concentration in America*, New York, NY: Oxford University Press, Inc. Retrieved from https://books.google.ca/books?id=Kd_1STqyGFcC&pg=PA194&lpg=PA194&dq=1992+personal+computer+market+idc&source=bl&ots=5s5eNwuf2u&sig=Ik7o5-JHyp6SfcZeBzLCdOotoqE&hl=en&sa=X

NTT, "NTT Positioned as a 'Challenger' in the Gartner Magic Quadrant for Global Managed Security Service Providers," 2014. Retrieved from http://www.marketwired.com/press-release/ntt-positioned-as-challenger-gartner-magic-quadrant-global-managed-security-service-nyse-ntt-1889307.htm.

Pandya, Mukul, & Shell, Robbie, *Lasting Leadership*, Upper Saddle River, New Jersey: Wharton School Publishing, 2005. Retrieved from https://lib.nu.edu.sa/uploads/m1/40.pdf.

Payne, Graham, and Allen, Brandt, *Dell Computer: Business to Business Over the Web*, Charlottesville, VA: Darden Business Publishing, 1999.

Pezzini, Massimo, Natis, Yefim, Malinverno, Paolo, Iijima, Kimihiko, Thompson, Jess, Thoo, Eric, Guttridge, Keith, "Magic Quadrant for Enterprise Integration Platform as a Service," *Gartner Group Research Report,* 2015. Retrieved from http://www.gartner.com/technology/reprints.do?id=1-2C8JHQO&ct=150325&st=sg.

Porter, Michael, *Competitive Strategy: Techniques for Analyzing Industries and Competitors*, New York: Free Press, 1980. (Republished with a new introduction, 1998.)

PriceWaterhouseCoopers, "MoneyTree Report Historical Trend Data," 2014. Retrieved from https://www.pwcmoneytree.com/HistoricTrends/CustomQueryHistoricTrend.

Reader, Ruth, "IDC: Tablet Shipments Decline for the First Time in Q4 2014," 2015. Retrieved from http://venturebeat.com/2015/02/02/idc-tablet-shipments-decline-for-the-first-time-in-q4-2014-leaders-apple-and-samsung-both-lose-market-share/.

Rivkin, Jan, "Revitalizing Dell," HBS No. 9-710-442, Boston, MA: Harvard Business School Publishing, 2010.

Schatzker, Erik, "Michael Dell: 10+ Companies Have Asked for Advice on Going Private," 2014. Retrieved from http://www.valuewalk.com/2014/12/michael-dell-10-companies-asked-advice-going-private/.

Schultz, Randall, "Compaq picks new CEO," July 1999. Retrieved from http://money.cnn.com/1999/07/22/technology/compaq/.

Schumpeter, Joseph, *Capitalism, Socialism, and Democracy,* New York, New York: Harper & Row Publishers, Inc., 1950.

Schumpeter, Joseph, *The Theory of Economic Development,* (Harvard University, Ed.), Cambridge, MA, 1934.

Senge, Peter, *The Fifth Discipline: The Art and Practice of the Learning Organization.* New York: Doubleday/Currency, 1990.

Shontell, Alyson, "Here's How Long It Took 15 Hot Startups To Get 1,000,000 Users," 2012. Retrieved from http://www.businessinsider.com/one-million-users-startups-2012-1?op=1.

Sommer, Dan, "Gartner Says Worldwide Business Intelligence and Analytics Software Market Grew 8 Percent in 2013," 2014. Retrieved from http://www.gartner.com/newsroom/id/2723717.

Statista, "Average Selling Prices of Desktop PCs Worldwide," 2015. Retrieved from http://www.statista.com/statistics/203759/average-selling-price-of-desktop-pcs-worldwide/.

Strumpf, Dan, "U.S. Public Companies Rise Again," *The Wall Street Journal,* February 5, 2014. Retrieved from http://www.wsj.com/articles/SB10001424052702304851104579363272107177430.

Sutton, Robert, and Rao, Huggy, *Scaling Up Excellence.* New York: Crown Publishing Group, 2014.

"The State of the Tablet Market," *TabTimes,* 2015. Retrieved from http://tabtimes.com/resources/the-state-of-the-tablet-market/.

Tuckman, Bruce, and Jensen, Mary Ann, "Stages of Small-Group Development Revisited," *Group Facilitation,* 10, 43–48. Retrieved from http://gom.sagepub.com.ezproxy-library.ocad.ca/content/2/4/419.full.pdf+html.

Ubrani, Jitesh, "Worldwide Tablet Shipments Miss Target as First Quarter Experiences Single-Digit Growth," *IDC Research Report,* 2014. Retrieved from http://www.idc.com/getdoc.jsp?containerId=prUS24833314.

Ungar, Lyle. "Your iPhone is Going to Outsmart You," 2008. Retrieved from http://scienceprogress.org/2008/05/your-iphone-is-going-to-outsmart-you/.

Van der Meulen, Rob, and Rivera, Janessa, "Gartner Says Worldwide IT Spending on Pace to Grow 2.4 Percent in 2015," *Gartner Group Research Report,* 2015. Retrieved from http://www.gartner.com/newsroom/id/2959717.

Verrastro, Justin, "Report: Managed Security Services to Boast 15.4% CAGR Between 2013 and 2019," 2014. Retrieved from http://www.apextechservices.com/topics/articles/386238-report-managed-security-services-boast-154-cagr-between.htm.

Walls, Michael, and Dyer, James, "Risk Propensity and Firm Performance: A Study of the Petroleum Exploration Industry," *Management Science*, 42(7), July 1996. Retrieved from http://www. jstor.org.ezproxy-library.ocad. ca/stable/pdf/2634364.pdf.

White, Anthony, "Urban Dictionary: freak flag," 2006. Retrieved from http://www.urbandictionary.com/define. php?term=freak+flag.

Yarow, Jay, "Apple's iWatch Could Be Super Profitable for Apple," 2013. Retrieved from http://www.businessinsider. com/apples-iwatch-could-be-super-profitable-for-apple-2013-3.

Index

About the Author

HEATHER SIMMONS WORKED AT DELL in both Austin and Toronto for over 13 years, from 1992 to 2005. She led teams involved in some of Dell's greatest crises and triumphs, and had a front row seat for Dell's unprecedented growth in the '90s and sideways slide in the mid-2000s. A Certified Public Accountant and a Harvard MBA, she brings both a bean counter's eye for the numbers (the "hard stuff") and an insider's perspective on the cultural shifts (the "soft stuff") which contributed to Dell's performance. Prior to Dell, Heather worked for accountants Arthur Andersen & Co. and consultants McKinsey & Company. After Dell, Heather served as the CEO of a high-tech start-up and the chairman of a life sciences start-up. Her success rate with start-ups is running about 50%, and she wonders whether she should quit while she's ahead.

This book has been designed by Katie Meyer at
Murmurous Publishing in Toronto, Ontario. It was
printed by CreateSpace.

The typeface is Sabon Roman. The titling face is
Minion Pro.

The data visualizations are by author Heather Simmons
and were built in D3, a JavaScript
programming library.

The cover is by Dushan Milic.

Thank you for reading *Reinventing Dell* by Heather Simmons.

To talk to the author, you can reach her via @heathersimmons on Twitter.

To **schedule a book reading** with the author or make a bulk order, contact heathersimmons@murmuro.us.

Printed in Great Britain
by Amazon.co.uk, Ltd.,
Marston Gate.